TABLE OF CONTENT

REFACE

I have been reading Rumi's books for years and enjoying them enormously. In particular, Masnavi. I have used its stories and similes, repeatedly in my lectures and seminars. They have always been well received. However, when I began to treat a number of my patients by hypnosis and cognitive behavioural therapy, my views about Rumi changed. I realised Rumi's teachings, have a brilliant ability to be used as a tool in changing people, and his stories are full of the essential basis of hypnotherapy, to the extent that it makes the listener fall in a trance state.

Rumi assigns a key position to the transcendental state. The whole of the 6 volumes of Masnavi and Diwan-e Shams were composed with himself being in such a state.

The more I understood Rumi, the more I was affected by him. Gradually I began to use his stories, similes and comparative examples, in my cognitive behavioural therapy and hypnotherapy sessions. The result was incredible, although more than anyone else, it completely changed my own life. It also had the same effect on others who had taken up Rumi studies and put it into practice for problem solving. I, therefore, decided to write these findings in this book.

These studies strengthen two faculties in a person, namely, love and reason. Anyone who has sufficient abilities in the art of loving, and the administration and management of reason, is able to overcome any problems.

Rumi, by using the trance state and story telling, places key beliefs in the mind of the reader and the listener. Even though with hypnoses and methods in cognitive behavioural therapy, it is easier and faster to get to this state, I have mixed those methods with Rumi's teachings. In fact, the method presented in this book, is a mixture of Rumi's teachings with hypnotherapy and cognitive behavioral therapy.

Fariborz Arbasi, M.D.

ABOUT THE AUTHOR AND TRANSLATOR

ABOUT THE AUTHOR

Dr. Fariborz Arbasi, is a graduate from the Department of Medical Science of Kermanshah University in Iran. He has extensive experience in a wide range of areas of psychotherapy, in particular in, hypnotherapy, cognitive behavioural therapy in treatment of depression, anxiety, weight control, addiction and other unwanted habits.

He has put into practice Rumi's teachings and incorporated the same in seminars, lectures and workshops, on handling stress, problem solving, effective management, decision making, sound exercise of discretion, dependence and unwanted habits.

ABOUT THE TRANSLATOR

Dr Sherry Nabijou is a PhD graduate in Science and Engineering from Imperial College London. After a successful career in Civil Engineering, she diverted to humanity sciences and qualified as a lawyer. She is a practicing Barrister in England. She has studied for many years philosophy, spiritual sciences and gnosticism as a personal interest and is a student of Rumi for life.

PART I: RUMI'S TEACHINGS

ABOUT RUMI

Jalal Al-Din Mohamad Balkhy, known as Rumi (30th September 1207 - 17 December 1273), the greatest mystical poet of Persia, was born in Balkh in the Northern Persian province of Khorasan, now in Afghanistan. His family were settled in Balkh for several generations and were highly respected and had produced a notable succession of divines.

His father, Baha Al-Din Valad, was a respected, highly knowledgable and famous spiritual leader. When Rumi was 12, the family departed from Balkh, and after several diversions to their journey, they ended up in Rum (Turkey). They first resided in Zarandeh, where Rumi later got married and his eldest child, Sultan Valad, was born. Thereafter, they moved to Konia, where he lived for the rest of his life.

During the time his father was alive, he was taught by him and other eminent spiritual leaders. He soon became a spiritual leader himself, and after his father passed away, whilst he continued to be guided by a number of notable spiritual masters, he attained the rank of Shaykh in 1240 (also the title of Maulana given to him by his disciples, meaning "Our Master"). Thereafter, he continued with his teachings, and sermons and gathered disciples in ever increasing numbers.

In 1244, he met a wandering dervish by the name of Shams Al-Din of Tabriz. Through him Rumi was totally transformed. Shams was around for nearly two years altogether, and absent for over a year. In 1247, Shams disappeared without any trace. Rumi's most important ocean of philosophy and wisdom, composed in poetry, occurred after the final disappearance of Shams.

Rumi's works, in the main, consist of the celebrated Masnavi (epic poems), in six volumes and 25,000 rhyming couplets, Divane Shamse Tabrizi (Lyrics of Shams of Tabriz), consisting of 2500 mystical odes (35000 verses), the Rubaeeyat or the quatrains, of which 1600 are authentic, and his discourse, Fih ma Fih.

Professor Reynold A. Nicholson, a scholar at Cambridge University (1868-1945), who translated all the six books of Masnavi, refers to them as "in the most part showing Rumi as the perfect spiritual guide engaged in making others perfect and furnishing novice and adept alike with matter suitable to their needs". (A Rumi Antholgy, by R.A.Nicholson).

Rumi considers the most important duty for anyone to be that of attaining self-knowledge and living a happy tranquil life. According to Rumi, a happy life is achieved by the blossoming and growth of the the talents of each individual. He uses different tools, such as, stories, metaphors, similies, propositions, poems and the like, to teach this path.

CHAPTER ONE: RUMI'S PSYCHOLOGY

The two important branches of Persian Gnosticism are, Gnosticism emanating out of fear, and Gnosticism emanating out of love. In the former, as its name suggests, fear is the central element. For example, fear of unwanted and unhappy future, fear of falling into sinful acts, and the sort. Imam Mohammad Ghazali, who was the follower of this path, explained this beautifully in his book called the Alchemy of Happiness.

The Gnosticism emanating out of love, is based on the art of loving. This is beautifully explained in Rumi's Masnavi. Even though the aim of these two branches of Gnosticism, is the same, namely, happiness and a prosperous life, they use two strategies with different facilities and consequences.

The Fearing Gnosticism

Fear of retribution, fear of falling and being contaminated with dirty and nasty individuals and events, constitutes the foundation of this type of Gnosticism. Hence, the key practices of this path are refraining, discipline, austerity, worship and the like.

It should also be said that fear is not only limited to this type of Gnosticism. Today this strategy is used in education, politics, medical and employment fields, in order to create motivations. For example:

The students who study, because of fear of failing their exams.
The sportsman who fears failing in the tournament, and is motivated to keep fit by training, and exercising.
The employee who is in fear of losing his earnings, and goes to work every day.
The manager of a firm, who is in fear of bankruptcy, and gets motivated to put more effort in his company.

The existence of prison and different forms of punishments, are all symbols and signs of fear.
Fear is the source of many important motivations, which make a difference, and bring about success, progress and management.

Many problems, in the field of education, employment, finance, communications, and the sort, are created through lack of fear or suppressing it.

The secret of success in any field, is the ability to invest in future. If a person is not able to save, he will never have any wealth accumulated. Even if he wins the lottery, his wealth will not last. Consistent and good relationships, educational or career successes, all require investments. One of the most powerful elements, operating in all of us, is the fear of future, with the operation of foresight.

The bases of Ghazali's Gnosticism emanating from fear are:

1. Human beings are born with defects, and will not attain perfection except by making strenuous efforts and be cured.

2. Human beings are capable of learning, and change is possible by learning.

3. The way to perfection, begins with self-knowledge and the way of life.

4. Cleaning the mind of improper behaviour, such as anger, pride, selfishness, greed, etc

5. Bad behaviour in human beings are turned into habits, and eliminating these habits, and replacing them with good habits, is possible through austerity.

6. Obtaining good and proper qualities, such as resolutions, gratitude, worship, fear and hope, reflections, regrets, remembering death and the judgment day.

7. Looking after oneself by meditation, reflection, taking accounts and stock of the situations, and also remembering death.

Gnosticism emanating out of Love

The books of Imam Mohammad Ghazali and in particular the Alchemy of Happiness were sources which influenced Rumi's thoughts. This influence was such that, if anyone wants to fully understand the trend of Rumi's teachings in relation to psychology and anthropology, and the foundation of his Gnosticism, must read the Alchemy of Happiness first. Rumi, not only praised Ghazali, but also he used many of Ghazali's similes and stories in Masnavi.

Rumi accepts that one is able, with the management of reason and the "motivation caused by fear", to become successful, and to avoid diversions out of the path to perfection. However, he believes by using the faculty of love, we are able to progress faster on the path to perfection, with less danger of diversions.

Rumi compares, on many occasions, the motivation caused by love, and that caused by fear in symbolic stories.

Fear is no more than a thin strand of hair, compared to love,
All are sacrificed for love religion

Love has five hundred feathers,
Each measuring from the earth to the skies

The worshiper, hastes on foot ahead, under the operation of fear,
The lovers fly more readily than the current and air

Those who are in fear, will not even reach the dust raised by love,
As love flies in the skies (Rumi,Masnavi, book 5, part 87)

Rumi regarded three main weaknesses on the path motivated by fear, when compared with that related to love. These are, slowness caused by fear, potential and probable diversions out of the path, and the suffering whilst on the path.

Slowness

Fear is able to move us forward on the path of perfection. This is because the fearing man pays more concentrated attention to staying on the path and not getting diverted. Rumi says, the Gnostic, in each moment, flies to the beloved, whereas the fearing man progresses on the path in one month, the distance which should have taken a day.

Even though the progress of the worshiper's spiritual conduct is incredible,
Its daily efforts, are not equivalent to fifty thousand years' worth

The lover's daily efforts are equivalent to fifty thousand years' worth

The lover with each breath is at the king's thrown
The worshiper takes one month to progress one day's worth
(Rumi,Masnavi, book 5, part 87)

Diversion

The next event on the path is diversions. This is particularly noticed in those giving up addictions, or other destructive habits. In giving up any addiction, we face two motivations; first, is the motivation caused by the destructive behaviour or habit. The second, is the resistance against losing the habit, or taking on new activities.

Continuation of the past behaviour and taking on new activities, are related to balance between the two. When a person is able to see the effect of addictions and their consequences, the fear of those consequences, motivates him further to give up the addiction. However, by moving away from the situation which caused the fear, the colour of that, which caused the fear, become less pronounced, and the motivation emanating from fear is reduced further, and it goes out of balance with the benefits emanating from giving up the destructive habit or behaviour.

Soured-faced and serious

Fear is accompanied with emotions such as anxiety, worry, feeling of sinfulness, and the like. A fearful person experiences an accumulation of these feelings. They are generally soured-faced and serious, and do not really enjoy the path.

If you have fallen in love, seek beauty and not blessing
If you are soured-faced,, sit and see blessing (Rumi, Diwan-e Shams, Ode
2002)

Cognitive Behavioural Therapy

If we look at Rumi and Ghazali's psychology, from the standpoint of today's divisions of psychology, they are in the category of Cognitive Behavioural Therapy.

What is Cognitive Behavioural Therapy?

Cognitive Behavioural Therapy, "CBT", is a type of therapy which concentrates on thoughts, feelings, and behaviours. Discovering habits, thought models which result in unpleasant feelings, destructive behaviours, and correcting those habits, help people and sets them off in the direction of using constructive feelings and behaviours.

Extensive research in the field of CBT shows that, it is one of the most powerful methods of dealing with depression, addiction, anxiety and many other problems of the mind. The use of CBT is spreading and today it is used in treating stress management disorder, communication problems, anger management and the like.

History

The roots of CBT go back to ancient philosophy and in particular to Stoics. They believed that the reason for any emotional disturbance and disorder is due to the judgement of the person in relation to the incident. It was unrelated to the incident itself. They also believed that a moral and wise person would not get entangled with these types of disturbances.

There are different methods of the operation of CBT, even though their bases remain the same. These methods consist of mindfulness and hypnosis.

CBT covers a wide range of clinical and non-clinical needs. It is operated in a pleasant way with variety. Today, CBT is available in clinics, group sessions, workshops, seminars, self-helping books, and online.

Similarities of and Differences between, Rumi's psychology and CBT

CBT and Rumi's psychology, have many similarities, namely:

Rumi also believes that our emotional disturbances and our unhappiness are related to our take and view of the events and with the correction of our views; we will be able to treat the problems.

Rumi also makes extensive use of these tools, namely:

The use of similes, metaphors, propositions, comparisons, and the sort, which are similar to methods used in Acceptance Commitment Therapy, "ACT".

The use of different and wide-ranging stories, to cause the listener and reader to elevate to trance state, and the extensive use of ambiguity and pun in his poems which are similar to Ericksonian hypnotherapy.

The use of mindfulness, which Rumi uses extensively in different ways in his stories and metaphors. Guest House, is a clear example of this.

Differences

One of the important differences, is the existence of effective techniques to cure problems associated with the mind, such as conditioning, which has eased behavioural change compared to the past. However, the key and important difference in Rumi's psychology with the current cognitive therapy, is in the domain of love.

In CBT, similar to Ghazali, the central chord is fear. They concentrate in correcting the view taken by the individual, in relation to a particular event, which has caused the destructive behaviour. The individual is taught, how to be cautious and look immediately for errors in his thinking, and correcting them.
This is the same in areas associated with depression or addiction, and other mind related problems. In addiction, the person is taught techniques to deal with temptations and relapse.

I have used CBT for many years for the treatment of my patients and for consultations. I have seen its success and its weaknesses. The weaknesses in a "fearfulness" systems are particularly pronounced in addiction related problems. As fear is the central chord, those using the method fall repeatedly into relapse. They are fearful, suffer from anxiety and guilt, and are slow in their progress.

Since I became familiar with Rumi, I used his teachings in the treatment of my patients for various problems, such as depression, weight reduction, dependance, addiction, bipolar, etc. I named it CBT by Love. The results were incredible. The interesting point was that I used the same method to effect change in myself and others, with great deal of success.

Rumi's psychology, in combination with effective techniques in CBT, has created a powerful tool, for those interested or are in need. Fortunately, one can use this tool in different ways. The content of this book is one way of using these effective and powerful tools.

PART II: ABOUT THIS BOOK

What benefit could this book have for you?

✓ Improves your emotional intelligence

Success in any areas or activities be it in leadership or management, in the field of economy, sport, politics or society, or in having a healthy relationship at home or at work, is attributed to the level of the operation of the emotional intelligence.

The emotional intelligence, is the ability to determine, weigh, and control emotions and feelings in oneself and others. Fortunately, this intelligence improves and its operational level is increased with exercise and training.

✓ Makes your cognition precise

Cognition, resulting in wrong analysis of the events, brings with it, amongst others, depression, wrong decision making, financial loss, etc. With improving sound cognitive powers, not only the person's behaviour is corrected, but also the other difficulties facing him, such as, depression, wrong decision makings, fear, and the like, are lessened or eliminated.

✓ Improves the ability to handle stress

Stress is one of the main obstacles facing people, on the path to success and making effective change. Anyone who is capable of handling stress properly, would be a more successful person in whatever he or she is doing.

Who can benefit from this book?

Those who want to change their unwanted habits, at personal level related to growth, addiction, and relationships, or in financial, or sociological related matters, and the like.

Those who want to change the operation of their emotions.

Those who have an ideal model can change and conform to that ideal.

CHAPTER TWO: HOW TO USE THIS BOOK?

This book has three main sections; the scrolls, exercises and tables. The seven scrolls consist of stories and Rumi's metaphors, similes and poems, related to love and reason. The exercises are related to self-hypnosis and cognitive behavioural therapy. The tables are presented for those who want to put into practice the teachings in the book, and are related to the scrolls and the exercises.

The readers can use this book in whichever way they like and home into the sections they enjoy most. If an individual wants to put the teachings of this book into practice, it is best to follow the guidelines provided.

Trance state and Conditioning

One of the most effective ways of changing one's beliefs is reading and listening to stories and metaphors whilst in a trance state, particularly at night, and putting into practice the essential points of the stories during the daily activities. This is a successful method, which has been used for thousands of years by various religions and schools of thought.

Another successful method is the technique of conditioning, which is used in cognitive behavioural therapy. In this technique, as soon as the person feels a negative emotion, he or she replaces it with reasonable thoughts, thereby removing the cause.

In this way, he is able to control the behaviour which had caused the disturbance. This replacement process, can take place alone, or in group sessions. Gradually, the person gets used to this method and the inappropriate behaviours and negative emotions disappear.

In this book, two powerful tools, namely, trance state and conditioning, are used as a mixture, in order to bring about change.

Trance State

Trance state is a state of awareness with two specific characteristics. One is deep concentration on the specific subject being addressed, accompanied by reduced attention to surrounding matters. The other is being in a state of high suggestibility and acceptability. Hence, the person is highly concentrated and easily suggestible.

Many of us, during our daily activities, experience light and at times, deep, trance state. When we are watching a sport tournament, or are excited watching a film, or are drowned in enjoyable, fearful, depressive, or joyful ...... emotions, or even taking a shower, or having an ice cream, a simple trance state is experienced.

 The interesting point is that the person by going into a trance state, automatically moves into the sub-conscious. This is because, trance state, is the gateway of entry to the sub-conscious, and many real changes occur in this realm, or in the world of sub-conscious.

The subject matter of the scrolls, together with short stories, poems, propositions and similes, not only will deepen the trance state, but also will leave their effect in the sub-conscious.

Conditioning

Marking the tables daily, places the reader in a (half) conscious state. In this state, the reader by observing his or her destructive habits will gradually transfer them from the sub-conscious to the conscious level. This way, he or she is able to weaken them and gradually eliminate them. Further, by doing the conditioning exercises daily, the reader is able to turn new, good and useful behaviour, into his or her habits.

SCROLLS

The purpose and the aim of reading the scrolls is to strengthen the faculties of love and reason. As mentioned before, essential truth, capable of strengthening love and reason, are presented in the form of metaphors, stories, poems, and purposeful propositions.

These beliefs surpass the self-awareness state of the reader and place themselves in the subconscious. The reader with daily observation, contemplation, and measured thoughts, feelings, and behaviour, is able to be assisted by this process. Also, it creates a helpful model within the mind which assists in strengthening the faculties of love and reason.

The number of Scrolls

There are seven scrolls, namely:

1. Polishing

Love
2. Attention

3. Wanting

4. Dying

Reason
5. Cognition

6. Management

7. Harmony

The three scrolls of attention, wanting and dying are related to specific qualities of love, and the three scrolls of cognition, management and harmony are related to specific qualities of reason. Polishing is a necessary prerequisite of love.

Method of work

Each exercise table is designed for 14 days. Each table, has 3 questions, which should be answered three times a day.

Each question has a mark ranging from 0 to 3. At the end of each day, the marks are added. The maximum mark in two weeks is 210. If one is able to score 150 in two weeks, he or she can then be ready to go to the next scroll. If the total is less, the same scroll is repeated.

The main aim of reading the scrolls, doing daily observation and marking the tables, is replacing beneficial beliefs into the system and obtaining necessary skills. This aim will only be achieved, if the work done is with accuracy and honesty.

Monday	Date	Total scores: 12	AM	Noon	PM
Did I read the Polishing scroll?			Yes	Yes	Yes
Did I observe prejudicial behaviours in me?			No	Yes	No
Did I observe myself being greedy?			Yes	No	Yes
Did I do the conditioning exercises?			Yes	Yes	Yes
Did I do the palace exercises and self-hypnosis?			Yes		

CHAPTER THREE: THE POLISHING

Rumi believes, love is the faculty by which human beings are perfected. However, people only become aware of the true extent of their capabilities and faculties when they need them. When a person is sick, he seeks help by going to see a doctor and taking medication. People move towards wealth or a better standard of living, when they experience poverty or a lack in their life style. We get onto the path to perfection when we see a need in ourselves for improvement, development, progress or a want to eliminate defects.

There are many factors and causes which weaken the need in us, to develop towards perfection. The main causes are: prejudicial beliefs, greed, dependance, emotions and desires.

These causes, not only prevent us from truly seeing and cognising the situations and events, but also they act as veils preventing proper and true interaction between us and the universe. They keep us within the walls of limiting beliefs, emotions, and habits. Rumi gives an interesting simile in relation to this. He says: in each of us is an inner mirror capable of reflecting and showing us the perfected image. This mirror is stained by prejudicial and limiting beliefs, greed, vengeance, negative emotions and the like. This prevents us from proper sight and true interaction with the inner mirror. In order to be able to truly see, we must polish this inner mirror. It is worth noting that in the past mirrors were made of iron. When they got rusty they were polished.

Polishing the inner mirror is achieved by various means. Rumi regards, amongst others, awareness and increased levels of consciousness, austerity and personal discipline, detachment from uncontrolled thoughts and emotions, reasonable and ordered thinking, loving, experiencing failure and turmoil, as means by which polishing of the inner mirror takes place. He also regards reading Masnavi, and books of similar nature, a means by which the cleansing of the soul takes place, resulting in increased levels of happiness and all round prosperity.

In the scroll of polishing, the reader by reading and doing the daily exercises will be polishing the inner mirror. Readers can also use the exercises in Mindfulness for this purpose.

THE POLISHING SCROLL

With love we can overcome any obstacle, reach any goals and make any great dreams come true.   Love begins with seeing, but the problem is that we don't see!

Greed, prejudice, dependence, addictions and the like, block the path to sight. Even though the world is full of beautiful objects of love, treasures and golden opportunities, we are not able to see them, if the screens are not cleaned and polished.

Clean your eyes, from the hair of defect,
So that you are able to see the hidden garden and the evergreen orchard

Take out from your ears, the cotton wool of uncertainty,
So that the sound of the eruption from the sky, comes to your ears

Eject from the head and the nose, the mucus of cold,
So that heavenly breeze comes through your smelling sense

Don't allow any traces of fever to remain,
So that you can find the sweet taste of the universe (Rumi, Masnavi, book 2, part 40)

Rumi regards the world as rich, filled with goodness, beauty, and anything we need.

All we need to do is to clean our eyes, ears, and mind of rigid and prejudicial beliefs, so that we are able to feel the beauty of nature, wonders of music and the refreshing scent of the world. He believes that the fabric of the world is such that it gives us whatever we want.

There are a number of causes which affect our perception, separate us from good fortunes and growth, and hinder our abilities. These are:

Rigid and prejudicial beliefs
Greed
Emotions and Desires

RIGID AND PREJUDICAL BELIEFS

One of the reasons for inability to see the reality, is having prejudice. Prejudice and being rigid in one's beliefs is not limited to having ideologies. Anyone who is not able to look at a subject from the standpoint of another, suffers from prejudice.

Anyone in this state, looks at events wearing glasses which signify that prejudice. Hence, he or she is not able to see the reality of the situations.

In front of your eyes, you held a dark blue glass, Hence the whole world appeared dark blue

Unless you are blind, know this dark blueness is coming from yourself,
speak ill of yourself and no one else (Rumi, Masnavi, Book 1, Part 72)

Rumi regards prejudice as a sign of lack of growth and maturity. Taking a hardline, rigid attitude and having prejudice is being immature, like a child. A mature and wise adult does not hold beliefs by or with prejudice. He lives in the present moment and sees every moment as fresh and new.

Prejudice and taking hard line attitudes, is being immature,
Whilst in mother's womb, all is done is drinking blood (Rumi,
Masnavi, Book 3, Part 49)

Just as those suffering from prejudice, behave towards those
who disagree with them with anger and hostility, not
allowing them to present their opinion, the prejudicial beliefs in
our own mind also react in the same way.

A person having prejudicial thoughts and beliefs takes any
opposing view as a threat, as he is dependant on and is a slave
of his thoughts and beliefs. Hence, he considers the elimination
of that belief or thought to be the same as losing himself
and his identity.

Many people are a slave of their thoughts,
Due to this they are bored and sad (Rumi, Masnavi, Book 2,
Part 103)

Hence the person, who operates under prejudice, is constantly
in a state of denial, rather than facing reality. The screen
caused by his prejudice stops him from properly growing and
achieving progress. It makes him weak.

GREED

Another element which causes lack of sensitivity and inability to see is greed.

Rumi uses a simile of a greedy person and a duck, who is constantly pecking and collecting.

The greedy duck came with its beak in the ground, wet and dry, seeking what is buried

That throat did not waste a moment, hearing no other orders, but "eat" (Rumi, Masnavi, Book 5, Part 2)

He is like a thief who has trespassed into a house, and quickly fills up his bag without paying much attention to that, that he collects. Both valuables and not so valuables are collected in haste. He is busy collecting goods in such haste, as though, he anticipates another thief any moment, to arrive and take the goods.

In order to grow, we need air, water, food, sex, money, relationship, peace, personality, excitement, power, social credit, and etc. However, if we pay too much attention to any of these, so that they divert us from our plans for achieving our goals, we will be in a state of greed.

For example, a person has a boat, and his plan is to put the boat in the sea and go to a specific island. Everyday, before taking the trip, he has the boat serviced, and has its engine checked. The following day he does the same, and the day after and the one after that. He repeats this daily. If he does not do that one day, he would be bored.

His neighbour also has a boat and uses it everyday to burn oil. Another everyday eats in the boat. These people have all forgotten the real purpose of the boat which was to sail in the sea.

In fact, greed is a type of excess and indulgence. This indulgence operates in collecting wealth, enjoyment, consumption, fame, power, etc .It gradually changes the person, to the extent that the object of greed, whatever it may be, becomes the beloved and replaces the main objective and purpose.

Blossoming of the talents give their place to the subject matter and the operation of greed. Greed replaces love, and the person loses his sensitivity to growth and to his freedom. Instead he becomes sensitive to the loss of that, that he is collecting.   At the end, greed is transformed into an idol which gives the person direction and form. A greedy man becomes the slave of this idol.

Greed had designed your conduct,
Once it goes, you can see the dark bruised ugliness of your work (Rumi, Masnavi, Book 4, Part 44)

As the heavy idol becomes the focus of your life,
You became cursed and blind (Rumi, Masnavi, Book 3, Part 125)
Greed, in the history of mankind, arises by ignoring reason, has caused destruction to man. Any greed which began out of choice, is ended with addiction. The addicted man gradually is changed into a dry tree, which no longer lives, grows, or has greenness. It is like a leader, whose addiction to power, has dried his ability to see the reality of the situations and to have proper and correct judgment. He then, with his foolish decisions, carries his followers to the edge of destruction.

All the destruction of predecessors, s due to taking sandal wood as oud (Rumi, Masnavi, Book 4 Part 64)

They could see the difference, as it was apparent, and yet greed made one blind and deaf

As greed is capable of covering reason, what wonders if it turns its back to logic

Greed makes one blind, foolish and ignorant,
it makes death easy for the fools (Rumi, Masnavi, Book 5, Part 121)

Greed makes you run in vain towards the mirage, reason says look properly, it is not water

Greed overcomes one, as though it is the soul, The shouts of reason at that time are hidden

Until he falls in the pit of pride,
then it would hear blames from wisdom

Since his false inflammation was burst by the strings of the trap,
the rebuking soul began to blame him

Until the walls of destructions have not fallen on him,
he is not able to hear the counsel of the heart with his deaf ears (Rumi, Masnavi, Book 5, Part 81)

In truth, a greedy man does not make decisions in accordance with the reality of the situations and the changes which have taken place. The basis of his decision making is his idol. This is why the greedy man sees the mirage as real.

This wrong vision will drop him in one of the pits of financial turmoil, destruction of relationship, back breaking defeats, disturbance of his mental set up, and many other problems. These defeats, disturbances and turmoils are his opportunity to gain self-awareness.

The Greedy Ant

The ant gets so excited over a single grain, because he is not able to see the containers with tons of grains in them. He takes away that grain with fear and greed. The owner of the containers says: Oh you! As you are unable to see, you think the containers don't exist. You have seen from our containers just a single grain, to the extent of that, you have wrapped your body and soul around it.

Oh you, an insignificant drop, look at skies, go along like a lame ant, but look at Solomon

You are not this body, you are that beheld vision,
You will be freed from the body, if you have seen the soul

A person is all vision, the rest is flesh and skin,
What ever his eyes have beheld, he is that (Rumi, Masnavi, Book 6, Part 25)

The inability to see the bigger picture, will cause us, like the fearful ant, to get stuck to a worthless grain.

The inability to see the big opportunities would make me be dependant on my small opportunities, like a conservative fearful man.

The inability to see unlimited wealth, will cause me to be stuck to the little bit of money I have. Equally, with not seeing those great dreams, my little aims and goals become very important to me.

In closing my mind to the very many creative ideas, I make my single unripe idea to become the island of my dreams. Inability to see the possibilities of the future, causes us to get stuck to the past.
Inability to see unlimited identities causes me to take the single garment of my identity as myself.

EMOTIONS AND DESIRES

Rumi also attributes one of the obstacles to seeing, as being ruled and /or overcome by emotions.

If you are mean-hearted due to disputes, you view the whole world meanly

If you are happy as your friends desire,
this world appears to you as a flower orchard (Rumi, Masnavi, Book 4, Part 90)

As thoughts affect emotions, emotions can affect our beliefs and judgments. If we are happy, we become positive in our outlook, and as Rumi says, we see the world as beautiful and vice versa.

Desires and intentions also, like "controlling emotions" are turned into veils. The one viewing with a particular purpose cannot see the reality.

When intention appears, virtues become hidden,
a hundred veils from the heart go to cover the eyes

If the judge allows bribery-gain to hold his heart,
how could he distinguish the wrong doer from the victim
(Rumi, Masnavi, Book 1, Part 12)

Not seeing the reality will occur when reason is not operating from it's position.

By moving reason to one side, prejudicial beliefs, greed, dependence, addiction, and the like, cause the person to see, only what he desires, and not the reality.
In all these circumstances the person is a slave and is not
free. He is a slave of his thoughts, greed, addiction and

emotions.   This slavery is of such nature, that the person even forgets he is a slave.

Your companion is not me, is my shadow, my rank is higher than thoughts

When I have surpassed the thoughts,
I have become a swift traveler outside the thoughts

I am the ruler of my thoughts, and not ruled,
Because the builder is the ruler, not the building (Rumi, Masnavi, Book 2, Part 103)

We become the slave of our thoughts and emotions when we are under their control.   But when we rise above them, guided by reason, and view ourselves without judgment, we conquer them.

Self-awareness, is like shining a light at the domain of thoughts and make the bars of the prison apparent. When a person is going through turmoil and facing serious defeat, opportunity will arise for this prison to be destroyed, and the person is able to see the reality.

From today I do not look at turmoils and defeats in my life as negative. There are only two possible causes for them to have occurred.   Either the main cause of the problem is myself holding such view and this problem is as a result of my habitual thinking, acting, denial, running away from problems, etc., such as, bankruptcy or failing an exam...... Or I am not the cause, such as, natural disasters.

In the first scenario, there is an opportunity for seeing one's own deficiency and acceptance of reality and freeing oneself from slavery of those habits which has caused such deficiency.

Anyone, who is able to see his own deficiency,

Is galloping on ten horses in haste, in perfecting himself

(Rumi, Masnavi, Book 1, Part 149)

In the second scenario, with appropriately facing the problems, I become stronger than the past, as each problem and its solution is an opportunity for personal growth.

A calm sea does not train a skilful sailor.

The story of the Greeks and the Chinese

Rumi gives an interesting example in relation to polishing. He says, we all have our soul, a mirror, which we are able to see the face of the beloved.

A mirror in external form is made up of iron,
The mirror revealing the image of the soul is very valuable

Mirror, is the soul of the face of the friend,
The face of that friend from that Land (Rumi, Masnavi, Book 2, Part 1)

But when the mirror gets dusty and rusty (in Rumi's time they made mirrors out of iron), we are not able to see the image reflected in it. In order to be able to see the image, the mirror has to be polished.

Rumi in the story about the Greeks and the Chinese explains this beautifully. The Greek and the Chinese artists each claimed they were better than the other. The king invited them to compete with each other.

The Chinese suggested painting a wall and said they will paint one, and the Greeks can paint the other. The walls were facing each other. The Greeks, who were more clever and skilful, accepted. They set up a screen between the walls and began to work.

The Chinese were hastily going back and forth to the Palace and getting different colour paints and carried on with painting the wall. The Greeks did not get any paint at all and did not draw on the wall either. They only polished the wall.

They closed the door and continued to polish, Like the sky, it became pure and smooth

There is a path from two hundred colours to colourlessness, Colour is like the clouds and colourlessness is like the moon

Whatever splendour you see in the clouds,
know that it comes from the stars, the moon and the sun
(Rumi, Masnavi, Book 1, Part 157)

When the time of judgment came, the Chinese where playing their drums, as they were so happy with their art work. When the king saw the beautiful paintings on the walls he congratulated them.

The Greeks then pulled the curtains up. The king then saw the beautiful paintings of the Chinese and his own astonished self on the wall. The Greeks with continuous polishing of the wall, had turned it into a mirror.

The Greeks, O father, are those Sufis without study, book and theory,
As burnished and polished their mind cleaned of greed, jealousy and hatred (Rumi, Masnavi, Book 1, Part 157)

Old and dated beliefs, unreasonable and illogical emotions, habits, dependencies, etc., are like the dust and the rust on the mirror of the soul.

Your perception is the measure of your view of the world and its understanding,
The screen covering the pure, is your impure sense

Wash your senses with pure and clear water,
Know that the garment- washing of the Sufis, is like this

Once you have become purified, the screen would be taken off,
And the pure soul would attach itself to you (Rumi, Masnavi, Book 4, Part 91)

With the daily washing of the mirror, of identifications, beliefs and value judgments, it would remain clean and polished. Whilst motivated, see the beloved as new, and continue with the procedure of transformation into becoming the beloved.

PART III: LOVE

According to Rumi, the faculty of love has special and effective abilities. For example, he calls it a horse with wings, which is capable of taking one to the beloved with the speed of light.

Like the horse with wings, love was the saddle on which we were riding,
We turned, and sped away to the skies (Rumi, Diwan-e Shams, Ode 1595)

Love is an alchemy which brings out our positive talents. It makes us grow.

Love is the alchemy of the alchemy maker, It turns soil into a treasure of Meanings

At times, it opens the doors to the unbounded skies, At others, from reason, it makes a ladder

At times, it puts forth a happy gathering with wine, At others, it gives the gifts of pearl like sea

At times like Jesus it cures the sick,
At others, like Abraham is hospitable (Rumi, Diwan-e Shams, Ode 822)

Be joyful, O our dear Love,
Oh you, the healer of our sickness

O, you dear love, the medicine for our selfishness and our fame-loving,
Oh You, Our Plato and our Galen

Anyone whose clothes were torn by loving, Is cleaned of greed and all sicknesses

When love is not his or her motivation,
He would be like a featherless bird, what a pitiful state! (Rumi,
Masnavi, Book 1, Part 1)

Rumi regards loving as an art and a skill which is capable of being taught.

SPECIAL QUALITIES OF LOVE

Analysis of Rumi's works, reveals three pronounced special qualities in love

Attention
Wanting
Dying

Attention

Attending to the beloved, and the motivation and energy needed to move towards him or her, creates the basis for becoming him or her.

Rumi believes it is possible to detect the object of people's attention, from their behaviour. People turn into that they attend to.

The Wanting

Rumi regards wanting like a cock crowing, announcing the coming of the morning, and bringing the good news of the achievement of one's goals.

He says, whenever we honestly and happily, with proper motivations, want something, we should be rest assured that we would get it, as the true seeker, is also a finder. According to him, thinking, emotions, acting and our activities, are all different forms of wanting.

Dying

Arriving at and transforming into the beloved, is the start of a new life. There is no new life without the death of the old life. On this basis, death has a key role in loving.

Rumi, calls this type of death, death by transformation, just like a child turning into a young man , and then a man. As lovers are always growing, they are constantly born and die of this type of death.

CHAPTER FOUR: THE ATTENTION

Paying attention is one of the key subjects in cognitive psychology. Anyone who wants to change, necessarily will attend to the subject of attention.

Sellers, writers, leaders, politicians, clergies, tutors, psychologists, journalists, poets, parents, teachers, or anyone with ideas, goods or services to present or sell, would be involved with the subject of attention. Success very much depends on the ability to keep the focus of attention of our listener on what is being presented. This is because attention creates motivation, and if anyone wants to strengthen, weaken or change the motivation of another, he must change the subject matter of that person's attention.

Changing the subject matter of attention and creating motivation, is not just the domain of the leaders operating in group activities. Anyone who wants to make changes in him or herself, also needs them.

Paying attention, not only provides us with the necessary fuel for the path to change, but also in itself causes change. Deterministic choice of the subject matter of our attention can change our mind image.

We all have a mind image of ourselves, and in accordance with that image, we have various beliefs about ourselves. Self confidence, views, abilities, goals and dreams, place us in direct contact with this self image in our minds.

Our mind image can be limiting, weak or vulnerable, or it can be able, positive and progressive, and blossoming our capabilities and talents. The good news is that the mind image is capable of changing. Mind images solidify if they are being continuously attended to. When they are not, they are weakened and withered.

One of my interests is to read biographies. In majority of biographies I have read, I noticed that sustained change took place in the person, when he or she paid particular attention to a model.

In some cases, such model was a historical, sports, religious, sociological, arts, etc. personality, and in others it was the ideal-self of the person himself. When attention to a model is given and is sustained, gradually that model replaces the image in the person's mind, and the consequence of this replacement is, changes in the person's thoughts and emotions, and finally behaviour.

This is why Rumi considers the first lesson in loving to be seeing and attending to the beloved.

The scroll of attention, with the aid of stories and metaphors, deals with the strengthening of that aspect of change related to the deterministic choice of the subject matter of attention. The readers, by reading this scroll and doing the corresponding exercises effectively change their mind image.

THE ATTENTION SCROLL

Seeing is the starting point of love and attention is its continuation.

Attention does two important works in love:

1. It creates a need in the lover, and the need creates motivation and action.
2. It begins the alchemy of the transformation of the lover into the beloved.

NEED AND MOTIVATION

The act of loving is to open that window,
Because the mind is illuminated from the beauty of the friend

So look incessantly at the face of the beloved, This is in your hand, O my dear, listen

Make a path to your inner-self,
Ignore the thoughts, concerned with anything else (Rumi, Masnavi, Book 6, Part 94)

Loving is to open the window to the beloved and watching him or her. Each traveler needs some bag-packs for the journey. In the journey of love, I get my bag-packs and energy from looking at the beloved, as attention creates my needs, and my needs motivate me, and motivation puts me in action, and action determines my destiny.

Action is born out of thoughts. Attending to anything rejuvenates energy and that energy creates emotions and behaviour. If attention is weakened, emotions and behaviour emanating from that attention also weakens.

If attention is stopped, emotions and behaviour also stop. In fact, we feed our emotions and behaviour by paying attention to them and make them lasting.

Whatever we pay more attention to, that thing appears in our thoughts and feelings. In fact thoughts and feelings are our inner mirror. If you want to know, to what a person is internally attending to, take notice of his behaviour.

Emotions and thoughts are more accurate evidence of the understanding of the inner thoughts of people as opposed to their words. Rumi, beautifully explains this in the story of the misrepresenting man and the lying camel.

The story of misrepresenting man

A person wearing torn clothes came back from Iraq after a long period of absence. Friends asked about his absence. He said: I was the guest of a king and he gave me many gifts, and constantly praised me.

His friends said your appearance and poor state is evidently showing your lies. No hat and no proper clothing. Where is the sign of your friend, the praises and his gifts? If you are speaking well of that king, your appearance is complaining.

If your words are praising the king,
your entire appearance is complaining (Rumi, Masnavi, Book 4, Part 66)

Wasn't the king generous enough to give you a pair of shoes and trousers?

He said: the king gave me lots of clothes, but I gave them to the peasants.

They said: very well, we assume you gave all the gifts away, why are you in this bad state? What is the cause of your low mood?

A hundred upset in you, like thorn,
how could sadness be the sign of happiness

Where is the sign of love, faith and satisfaction?
if what you have told us be true (Rumi, Masnavi, Book 4, Part 66)

The lying Camel

One man asked a camel, "hey you, where have you come from?"

Camel answered, "From the warm bath of your
neighbourhood."
He said," this is apparent from the state of your dirty knees."
(Rumi, Masnavi, Book 5, Part 103)

If I am bored and not motivated, if I still continue with my destructive habits, it shows that I am attending to my ego.

Wean the child of your soul off, the devil's milk, Then, get it to
consort with angels.

Whilst you are dark, bored and gloomy,
know that you are co-milking with the cursed devil (Rumi, Masnavi, Book 1, Part 88)

My attention like my inner dialogue is turned into habits. To change this habit, it is sufficient to get onto observation.

Whenever I feel my excitement and motivations are lowered, feeling board or tempted, or at times of decision making, I go back to the window of the beloved and watch him or her. The change in the object of attention, is like making changes at source.

This type of change is both easier and brings about great opportunities. With a few small shovels, direction and path of a large river are changed.

With changes made to the objects of my attention, I change my behaviour and my destination.

THE ALCHEMY OF ATTENTION

Everyone has an image of himself in his mind which he day and night attends to.

With continuous attention, this image becomes clearer, takes up a life of its own to the extent that many take themselves as being this image.

If people move their attention from the image and direct it to another image, they would become like that other image. This is what happens when we pay attention to sports, arts, media, public or political figures.

Attending to the beloved, will replace the mind image of the lover with the image of the beloved.

The story of Majnoon and the letter

[Like Romeo (Majnoon), and Juliet (Laily)]

Majnoon wanted to write a letter to Laily. He picked up the pen and wrote as follows:

When you reside in me, so who should I write this letter to? Hence, he broke the pen and tore the paper. (Rumi, Fihi Ma Fihi, Chapter 44)

The main point in the exercise of loving is to see and to watch the beloved.

The lovers' teacher, is the overwhelming beauty of the friend, Their book, lesson and lecture, the face of the friend (Rumi, Masnavi, Book 3, Part 184)

The school is love, and the teacher is the overwhelming beauty,
and we are, the determined seeker of knowledge (Rumi, Diwan-e Shams, Ode 429)

Continuously look that way and rub your eyes,
because the school and the revision, is this, for your soul (Rumi, Diwan-e Shams, Ode 342)

We turn into that, which we attend to. I have always paid a lot of attention to myself. Hence, I became more and more like myself and stopped changing.

If like Majnoon my whole being is filled with the beloved, I would become the beloved.

From today I would replace my own image with the image of the beloved, and by continuous attention, the image would become greater and clearer, to the extent that the image of the beloved is the only image which I can see.

The story of Majnoon and pain

Majnoon got sick and a Doctor came to see him. After examining him the Doctor said he had to take a blood sample.

As soon as Majnoon felt the sharp tip of the needle, he shouted, "This was not necessary and even if I die I will not allow you to put this needle in me."

The Doctor said, "You go lion hunting, and are famous amongst all, for your bravery and courage. What are you afraid of?"

Majnoon said, "I am not afraid of the needle or the injury, but the whole of my being is filled with Laily."

But my whole being is filled with Laily,
This shell is filled with the qualities of that pearl

I am afraid of you injecting me,
you would sting Laily (Rumi, Masnavi, Book 5, Part 79)

Rumi says when you step in the path of love, then do not look at yourself, your individuality, values, pains and enjoyments. Only look at your abilities and to the beloved. Your ego, as is changing and vanishing, has no reality.

What is real is the beloved, which at any present moment you are attending to.

Do not look at the ugliness or the beauty of your role, See love and the object of your want

Do not look at your weaknesses,
See your abilities and intentions, O noble one (Rumi, Masnavi, Book 3, Part 53)

Attending to the beloved, not only in every moment I become new and am filled with energy, but also every day I am transformed into him or her. On the other hand, the chains of my slavery become stronger, if I continuously think about my ego (the present self).

From today I see in myself, the beloved (the ideal self), and nourish it by my continuous watching, thinking, and paying attention.

Inversely, in accordance with my habits, if I want to think of "present self", immediately I see me from the point of view of the beloved.

Once this new habit has replaced my old habit, I have become the beloved.

CHAPTER FIVE: THE WANTING

Rumi believes, if one wants something, it will be given. Probably this belief does not accord with our experiences, as many of us have wanted many things and have not fulfilled them. Rumi accepts that these disappointments occur, and believes one of the reasons for not getting what we want is because our wants are not pure.

Many people verbally or by thoughts want something, but their actions are not compatible with their wants. For example, someone wants a really fit, slim and healthy body, but his or her lifestyle is full of fast food, being immobile, and not doing any exercises. Wanting is not just by words or thoughts.

Each activity of ours, whether by words, thoughts or action is in fact a kind of wanting. The incompatibility in our wants, could be the incompatibility existing between our thoughts and actions. It could be incompatibilities in our beliefs, values, or even our conscious and sub-conscious.

I have many times, in the therapy sessions with my clients, observed these incompatibilities and impurities in their wants. Hence, the purity of the wants, is one the important factors of "proper and correct wanting".

Another important factor in a proper and correct want, is persistence in the wanting. Fulfilling the want, is not a single event. It is a process. Having a want on one occasion, and putting it on hold by sitting around and doing nothing to fulfil it, practically means "not wanting".

In order to fulfil any want, not only one must look after the fire of the need and the wanting, but also one must make the flames greater.

The third sign of the proper and correct wanting is to act with interest and motivation. Rumi believes, in order to fulfil our wants, we must make the effort with maximum motivation, interest and excitement, and not to stop making continuous effort until the desired result is achieved.

He, not only encourages motivations and exerting high levels of interest in our actions, but also he believes, wants expressed in words and by prayers must have the same levels of interest and motivations.

In this scroll, the readers, by observation over their daily activities, are able of making their wants more pure, more sustained and more intensified.

THE WANTING SCROLL

When, "attention" becomes extensive and deep, it is transformed into a "wanting".

Rumi attributes five specific characteristics to an effective wanting, namely, the Sign, Purity, Perseverance, Creativity and Maintaining.

THE WANTING IS A SIGN

Rumi regards the wanting as a sign for achieving! He believes, when the Universe wants to give one something, in the first place, it creates the need for that thing in one.

Whatever state you are in, keep the wanting alive, Want the water, Oh you, with dry lip

Because your dry lip gives evidence that it will reach the spring-source at the end

The dryness of the lip is a message from the water, which will certainly bring to us this anxiety (Rumi, Masnavi, Book 3, Part 53)

The thirsty longs for the refreshing water, Water is also yearning, "where is that water drinker?"

This thirst in us is pulling the water to us, We belong to it and it belongs to us (Rumi, Masnavi, Book 3, Part 212)

If there was no water, we would not have got thirsty. The wanting is a "Sign" of the existence of that thing which we are in need of. Thirst is the Sign of water, love is the Sign of the beloved, poverty is the sign of wealth, and disease is a Sign of health.

The existence of these needs, not only is the Signs of the final goals, but also is giving evidence as to how they can be achieved.

From today, I cherish my wants, and hasten the stress and the pain caused by my wants, to get to and achieve my goals earlier.

This wanting is like the cock, crowing at dawn, bringing the news of the coming morning

This wanting is a blessed motivation within you, in truth, it is the destroyer of obstacles

This wanting is the key to achieving your goals,
your army and the joyous victory proclaimed by your winning banners (Rumi, Masnavi, Book 3, Part 53)

Even though it is still night and darkness prevails, the sound of the cock crow, is bringing the good news of the morning.

I enjoy every moment of the coming of the morning. My wanting of today is like the turning of my key in the lock of problems. With motivation, joy and childlike enthusiasm, I open the door to my aims. My wants are my army and my power.

Today my army has no other choice but to be victorious, as their ships are burnt at the shore. From today, in order to achieve my goals and fulfill my dreams, the power within me will be like that of a flood, whereby all obstacles would be swept away.

Whenever I face an obstacle along the way, I am immediately grateful, as I would get stronger when I remove the obstacle.

THE PURITY OF THE WANTING

Whatever response we receive, whether by sight or by hearing, it is a reaction to our wanting.

This world is a mountain and our action a shout,
from the shouts, the echoes come back towards us (Rumi, Masnavi, Book 1, Part 9)

According to Rumi, we will only get the real answers, when our wanting is real and pure.

When we have a number of conflicting wants, the responses we receive are conflicting and confused.

People are constantly calling God's name,
This will not work as it is not done with full-hearted love

Each comes with a hundred needs in the heart,
This is not the religion of Love (Rumi, Masnavi, Book 6, Part 115)

We have many different wants, all the time. That, which conforms the conflicting wants into harmony, is love.

Love flames the want of the beloved, and decreases the effect of other needs, desires and wants. With continuous and persistent attention given to the beloved, I make the need for the beloved greater and more intense, until the flames of my wants motivate the whole of me, and making me the seeker of the beloved. I know the seeker is the finder, and one becomes that, which one seeks.

Whilst you are seeking the gem in the mine, you are the mine,
Whilst you are seeking a mouth full of bread, you are the bread

If you understand this secretive point, you would know:

You are that, which you seek (Rumi, Diwan-e Shams, Quatrain 1815)

Rumi in Fihi Ma Fihi says, each activity is a kind of a question and answer.

"The goldsmith testing the gold is asking of its purity, and the answer is whether it is pure or alloyed. Hunger is a question of nature, stating in the house of the body, there is a crack, give brick, give clay. The answer is take. Not eating is an answer that there is no need at present, the brick is not yet dry, and cannot put force on it.

A doctor taking the pulse is a question, and the throbbing in the vain is an answer. Examining the urine is an unspoken question and answer. To cast a seed in the ground is a question asking for growth of the crop, and the growing of the sapling is the answer, without words as the question was wordless. Every activity we do is a question and anything that happens, whether sad or happy, is an answer." (Rumi, Fihi Ma Fihi, Chapter 40)

Each word I speak and each act of mine is a want. If I have a want which is not fulfilled, it is probably because my acts are not compatible with my want. Just to want is not sufficient for living with awareness and consciousness.

The Universe is not just doing lip reading. It is also looking at my mind, heart, and limbs. I will only satisfy my needs and achieve the object of my wants, when my words, thoughts, feelings, and acts are compatible and are at one with each other.

PERSEVERANCE OF THE WANTING

Whatever state you are in, lame or limping, untidy and unmannerly, crawl towards and seek the beloved

In any state you are in, whether talking or silent, detect the scent of the king (Rumi, Masnavi, Book 3, Part 37)

In whatever state I am, whether depressed, fearful, or disappointed, whilst stressed or in turmoil, I remain motivated and determined to achieve my goals. I think, talk, and seek nothing else but my wants. Thirst has eliminated all my other desires and I don't seek anything but water.

In this path, don't rest or let go of your efforts until the last breath

As, even if there was only a single breath left to live, the union with the beloved could be yours

A drowning man suffering in agony, desperately tries to clutch at any straw

Being in fear of his head going under, he struggles moving about his limbs,
with the hope that one would get hold of his hand in peril

The Friend loves this level of turmoil and agitation,
Even struggling in vain is better than doing nothing and surrender (Rumi, Masnavi, Book 1, Part 92)

I make all the effort in my power in order to achieve my goals. Even if there was only a single breath left in me, I use it to take a step forward towards my goals. My actions in each step of the way in this, path to success, are like the efforts made by a drowning man.

CREATIVITY OF THE WANTING

Rumi believes that if you persistently knock on a door, it will open and as you begin the journey, the path becomes apparent.

If you step on the path, the way will be revealed to you
If you become nonexistence, existence will be conferred on you
(Rumi, Masnavi, Book 5, Part 50)

Rumi points to the story of Joseph and Zolaikha. Zolaikha had locked all the doors in the palace as she wanted to have intimacy with Joseph. All the doors were locked and there was no glimmer of hope for Joseph to escape.

But Joseph began to run, with all his might, towards the closed door and suddenly the door opened. Rumi believes that the wanting in Joseph was the cause of the door opening.

Though Zolaikha locked the doors on every side,
There appeared to be a hopeless situation for Joseph to try

The locks and the doors opened and the way appeared, Once
Joseph put his trust in God and ran

Although there are no obvious means of exits from the world,
We must run like Joseph

So that the lock is broken and the door appears,
And you will dwell in the placeless space (Rumi, Masnavi, Book 5, Part 50)

We sometimes are placed in situations where, there does not appear to be any way out, even a little glimmer of light is absent. Even in these situations I continue with my wanting and keep up the motivation towards achieving my goals.

When disappointments have darkened the inner self and have eliminated motivations, relying on the powers beyond myself, is a glimmer of light, which gives me the power to continue and move forward.

Moving forward with hope is not as important as pressing on when disappointed. The latter is life changing.

Relying on ones knowledge and abilities when imprisoned by disappointments, thickens the walls of the prison. It is with action that the path becomes open and apparent. It is with death that life begins.

Disappointment is in fact life saving blessing amongst negative emotions. Running when disappointed, is the loudest shout of a brilliant need, and a sincere wanting of freedom and revelation.

Being dissatisfied with my situation, elevates me and places me in a more agreeable situation. Like Joseph running in the dark, it shines a light and shows the way. With my efforts, every moment, I keep the way to success open.

MAINTAINING THE WANTING

The flames of wanting remains lit with action. With effort and action, we can enhance the wanting and make it more powerful.

Wanting is like an investment. Add more wanting to your wants to increase the stake, or else your investments would vanish. You are no less than the earth. The soil is turned over and over to allow crops to grow. If the soil is left unturned, it hardens.

Hence, when you detect a wanting in yourself, don't say, " what is the benefit of this wanting?"

You step onto that path and the benefits will appear. A person does not go to the shop for any other reason but to say what he wants. (Rumi, Fihi Ma Fihi, Chapter 60)

Avoiding action and causing delay, dries my motivations. It turns my need into a latent pain, and it leaves behind an imprisoned soul and a disappointed mind.

Hurriedly I act and give life to my motivations, flames to my needs, reality to my mind, and tranquillity to my soul. I would not take away the life from my wanting, by irrelevant conservatism and weak thoughts. I have experienced that the more I act, my wanting becomes richer and the fruit of my dreams become plentiful.

CHAPTER SIX: THE DYING

Many of us, when we think of death, imagine it to be dark, gloomy, cold and frightening. On the other hand a vision of life is happy, exciting and interesting. We also consider life and death to be different and separate entitie. Hence, in order to live, we avoid death. Rumi regards life and death, to complete one another, and to be inseparable.

Rumi does not consider death to be just the physically dying of the body. He regards it as having a much wider meaning. For example, the growing up of a baby to childhood, then onto being a youth and so on, losing wealth, losing credit, immigration and leaving home, going from one season to another, moving from the state of sadness to happiness etc., all are living and dying.

From Rumi's point of view, life is like a river in motion, which inside it continuously life and death occurs, and it is this continuos flowing of the fresh water in the river that, enables its maintenance.

Hence anyone who wants progress and development, should welcome this type of death, which Rumi calls, death by transformation. However, today we witness many people who are prisoners of their addictions, dependance, destructive relationships, poverty, harmful thoughts and habits, and yet are not prepared to lose their destructive habits and make changes in their behaviour.

Also there are people whose beliefs and habits are keeping them in poverty and social depravation, and yet are not prepared to lose their destructive habits and beliefs.

Rumi regards the reason behind the above, to be fear. Fear of losing and of dying. The desire to maintain life, is the strongest desire in human beings and animals. This desire looks after our life. It is this desire which has protected human beings to date. Just as we need to maintain our physical body to function and to live, we also like to maintain our mindset. This assists us to protect our identity.

Mindsets are matters such as our roles, behaviours, beliefs, opinions, emotions, nationality and home town, our political, religious, and sport's views, our partner, children and friends, our possessions and property, and many examples of the sort.

Hence to lose or even have a threat of losing, anything which jeopardises our identity results in shock, anger, low moods and depression. Hence, many of us, in order to prevent this from happening, we remain in our comfort zone and we lose the opportunities of progress, development and the self-blossoming of our talents.

The scroll of dying presents Rumi's alchemy by metaphors and effective stories. The reader learns to discriminate and choose between events which happen in life.

He or she will also learn to embrace the stresses caused by changes taking place and how to manage them. The reader, in this scroll, will see "lovers", as a model, who go out of their comfort zones all the time, and will begin to learn from these "experts in dying", who experience every moment of life as fresh and new, filled with beauty, freedom and power.

THE DYING SCROLL

Dying is one of the most important aspects of Love. Rumi specifically emphasises on dying. In his view, death and life are inseparable.

A child who is growing is constantly in the process of dying and living. Rumi sees every moment of life as new.

With each breath the world and us become anew, and we are unaware of this renewal

Life like a new stream flows through,
and it appears to be continuous (Rumi, Masnavi, Book 1, Part 69)

Rumi says our life is like a stream. The water in the stream is renewed every moment. The water passing is not the same water a moment ago. Every moment, new water arrives and replaces the old.

We, also, die every moment and take a new life every moment. We don't see these moment by moment changes, but they exist.

Rumi calls this type of death, death by transformation.

Not the type of death that you go in the grave,
The transforming death, which you go into the light

Soil became gold and the soil's aspects did not remain,
Sadness became joy and the sting of sadness did not remain
(Rumi, Masnavi, Book 6, Part 22)

Rumi emphasises on three aspects of death by transformation at

Emptiness of oneself
Handling pain and stress, accompanying death by transformation
Continuance of love with repetition of death

EMPTINESS OF ONSELF

Elevation begins with death. Death is creating emptiness,
Life is filling the space

Death is emptying the mind of useless beliefs and values, Life is consciously choosing beliefs and values

Death is clearing the forced written play, Life is newly writing a play

Death is leaving the old steps behind, Life is taking new steps on

Death is loosing and letting go, Life is getting and holding on

Death is prevalent to life,
If there was no death, there would be no birth

The story of the death of the lover

A lover was telling his beloved of all the suffering he had had to go through for his love, saying, I did this and that for you, I suffered a lot, I lost my wealth, I forgo my respect, my credit, I thought of you day and night, and so on.

His intention was not to say he had done her favours. His purpose was to show the beloved just how much he loved her. The beloved said, all these you have done are fine, but you have not done the most important thing.

The lover said what is that? The beloved said, dying and ceasing to be! You have done all these things, but you are still alive! You have not died. If you truly love me, die!

You have done all these things but you have not died, you are still alive,
Die if you are the truly life-loosing lover (Rumi, Masnavi, Book 5, Part 56)

Death by transformation frees us of the prison of ourselves. Until I die of being myself, I will not become alive as being the beloved.

Building

One man came along and was digging the ground, Don't do that! a fool shouted

What are you destroying this earth for, digging and disturbing it?

O, you fool, go and stop shouting, said he,
You should understand that a new building is built out of destruction

How can this soil be turned into a flower bed or a wheat field, if it is not turned upside down and disturbed?

*How can it become a cultivated land, green and fertile, if it is
not turned upside down?*

*Do we hit a skilful tailor for cutting the fabric, protesting, why
he cut the expensive material in pieces?*

*A building is not renewed,
if first, the old one is not destroyed* (Rumi, Masnavi, Book 4,
Part 90)

In order to be transformed into becoming the beloved, first the
mind image of ourselves, and then our beliefs and habits must
be eliminated.

Equally, we must also eliminate the whole of the play written
by others, and prepare the mind for writing our chosen play.

*Does anyone write on a paper, which has writings all over it?
Or plant a sapling in a forest packed with trees?*

*I will be looking for a blank piece of paper,
I will plant the sapling on a spot which nothing is already
planted there*

*O, brother! be that unplanted spot,
Be the blank white piece of paper* (Rumi, Masnavi, Book 5,
Part 77)

Death is the clearing of the land of our being, off of all the
vegetation and trees planted on it by others. From today I will
look for a white blank piece of paper for writing my chosen
play, and a clear piece of land for planting my chosen saplings.

We all have beliefs and habits. Over time, they are influenced
by other factors, such as, society, family, media, and the like.
This is then made up to a phenomenon, which we call "self".

Rumi says, "This is not you!" It is a stranger in you. Your true self will begin to be formed when you consciously choose your true self and create it, with love. The creation of the true self begins with the perception of the beloved, and will continue with repeated death and revelation.

Die, die, do not be afraid of this death,
As, if you elevate from this land, you will get to the skies

Die, die, cut away from the ego,
As, this ego is like a chain, holding you as a slave

Pick up the ax and search for the prison cell,
Once destroyed, you are all kings and conquerors

Die, die, for the beautiful king,
As, if you die for the king, you are all famous kings

Die, die, come out of the clouds,
As, if you do this, you are all the bright moon (Rumi, Diwan-e Shams, Ode 636)

Self or ego, is the creation of biological constraints, and other factors, such as, family, childhood and youth, society, life events, and generally anything else other than conscious choices at any given moment.

From today any conscious decision of mine would be like striking with an ax the wall of my ego prison.

Understanding the beloved

Death, not only makes us run away from the self and be transformed into becoming the beloved, but also it allows us to understand the beloved. Rumi believes that for proper understanding of anything, we must be transformed into becoming that thing.

Become the resurrection, perceive the resurrection, This is the necessary condition of seeing anything

If you are not transformed into that, you will not know that fully, whether that be, light or darkness

If you become reason, you will know reason is perfection,
If you become love, you will know love is light (Masnavi, Book 6, Part 22)

Story of a friend

A lover after searching for a long time finds the beloved's house and knocks on the door. The beloved says, "Who are you?"
The lover says, "It's me."
The beloved says, this is not the time for meeting as you are still raw!

Who can cook the raw, other than the fire of separation and distance?
Which will deliver him from this hypocrisy

The lover returns and for the whole year suffers being separated from the beloved and becomes ripe and cooked. He goes to the beloved and knocks on the door, full of fear and with proper manners.
The beloved asks, "Who are you? "
The lover says, "It's you!"

Now that you are me, O, I, come in
as there is no room in this house for two "I"s (Rumi, Masnavi, Book 1, Part 144)

HANDLING PAIN AND STRESS

Any change results in stress. This could be changes such as, moving a child from one school to another, or changing where one lives, or moving jobs, or even growing from the stage of childhood to youth and so on. They are all accompanied by stress.

People adapt to situations quickly, be it, a home, a job, the food they eat, life style or even their driving habits, their bed or their sleeping patterns. A person in all these situations, whether related to the actual physical place, such as the home or the place of work, or related to the mind, such as habits or one's image of oneself, feels a sense of comfort. This is why it is referred to as the comfort zone.

But, as soon as change occurs, it causes anxiety, as the new place is unknown to the mind, and the alarm bells of fear are sounded causing stress.

Some of these stresses are enjoyable and some are rather annoying and upsetting, even though they don't last a long time and gradually disappear. But there are some greater and more permanent stresses, such as, losing a partner, or a child, or contracting an incurable disease. In these circumstances people get into a series of staged responses.

These responses are fivefold, namely, shock and denial, anger, begging, depression and acceptance. Those who are facing death would also go through these stages. It also happens to those who have lost loved ones, or even lost a job, or have gone through separations.

This is because each separation is a type of death. In these circumstances most of the person's comfort zone would be subjected to pain. The stresses and anxieties emanating from leaving the comfort zone, create obstacles in the path of changing, and conquering the habits or addictions.

But I have found the way to remove these obstacles! And that is love!

There are many stressful situations.   For example, consider being in a physical fight, or seeing a seriously injured person bleed, or facing an armed criminal.   These situations are stressful for an ordinary person, but they are not as stressful for a professional boxer, a surgeon, or a policeman. Their job is to be placed in these situations. A boxer is in the ring to have a physical fight, and either he hits, or is hit by another. The surgeon's job is to cut and stitch the body of his patients in the operating room, and witness bleeding. The police officer's job is to chase and arrest criminals.

Hence these activities could be hugely stressful for an ordinary person, whereas for a professional they would be normal and at times even exciting.

The dying of lovers is not of a single type, Lovers die all the time

The lover has two hundred souls,
And each moment he sacrifices the lot (Rumi, Masnavi ,Book 3, Part 184)

Yes the job of the lover is to die and to become alive again. If I want to be a lover, I have to get used to this profession.

May be it will be stressful at first, but dying will also become a habit gradually. From today, I will taste death, not as a single experience but as my first work experience.

Greeting stress

Rumi believe, that not only we must not run away from stresses caused by change, but also we must greet them. He looks at this in one of his most beautiful poems.

He says when we are in this prison of self, we are weak, bitter, and depressed and when we destroy the walls of this prison, aided by love, we become strong, attractive and joyful.

That moment you are self-full, a mosquito can fell you, That moment you are selfless, you bring down an elephant

That moment you are self-full, you are a bag full of sorrow-clouds, That moment you are selfless, fog tears apart for you

That moment you are self-full, the beloved stays away, That moment you are selfless, the beloved sends you wine

That moment you are self-full, you are like an autumn depressed, That moment you are selfless, January appears like the spring

Rumi in the second part of the following line presents the way to leave the self by saying, become a restless seeker. Hence, becoming at one with restlessness embracing stress.

All your restlessness is because of your want for rest, Be a seeker of restlessness, so that rest comes to you

All your indigestion is because of your want for digestion, Abandon digestion, you can even digest poison

The reason for not achieving your dreams, is because of your search for them,
Stop the searching, and all your wishes will be granted

Love the suffering caused by the beloved, and not his or her affections,
So that, the hard to get beloved, falls madly in love with you
(Rumi, Diwan-e Shams, Ode 323)

Which one is more successful: the fighter who is excited and is happy to fight, or the one who likes to avoid fighting? The lover who wants to die, or the one who is afraid of it, and avoids it?

Conquering any habit and giving up any addiction, are accompanied with stress and unpleasant emotions.

Anyone who can handle and bear stress better, has a better chance of success,. However, anyone who consciously and lovingly goes to greet stress, will certainly succeed.

From today I stop looking for a calm beach in my life, and I bring in my heart, the sea of danger with great and high waves of stress.

From today I kick all claims to belongings and expectations, and eye to eye with the beloved, I step in the desert of my wants. In this barren land, a little salty water, is more valuable and tasty to me, than any other drink. I put down all my wishes and dreams, small and large, and choose the path which I must take and step into the dark, cold, windy and raining atmosphere, with no expectations for any results.

The world has many different faces. Sometimes the weather is spring like, green and beautiful, and sometimes autumn, with falling yellow leafs.

Sometimes life is in accordance with our wishes, and happiness is all around, other times it is full of headaches, pain and suffering. The one who only plays life when it is happy, would not last when times are hard. The one who sees life only through the window of difficulties, becomes a stranger with happiness and comfort.

Fortunate is the one who is growing. He is strong when crossing the hardened land, and happy when passing through the happy and pleasant land.

From today when I walk out of my comfort zone, when passing through any land I become in harmony with it.

When passing through the land dimmed with sorrow, I would not close my ears and eyes. When I look at sorrow with acceptance, I get its message, and its beauty becomes apparent to me.

When I am passing through land of happiness, I don't get tempted to reside there, as this pleasant and colourful land is also for passing. When I accept this, I taste its sweetness and I pass. I have passed through many lands before.

There will be other lands to come. Disappointments, loneliness, comfort, suffering, courage, kindness, and so on are the secrets of seeing the beauty of any land and acceptance and tolerance of them. From today, I will, with this awareness, pass the unknown lands, in order to arrive at the beloved.

PERSEVERANCE IN LOVING

Going towards the beloved and the continuous transformation is a process and not an accident.

Therefore, perseverance in progress whilst on the path of love, is the requisite condition for a successful arrival.

I am enchanted by the one who does not consider himself arrived at his destination,
when he is only at a traveler's lodge

You have to leave the lodges,
so that one day you arrive at the destination (Rumi, Masnavi, Book 1, Part 150)

Stopping when on the path of love, is to allow depression, anxiety and the seeds of greed, dependence and addictions, be spread into the system.

If you move out of the circle of lovers,
Your heart will die and you will become depressed

If you are the sun in the universe, you will become like dark clouds,
Or if you are the new spring, you will be like autumn

Like a bowl when empty, you float on water and dance,
Once filled, you go to the bottom of the pond and be motionless

God gave you two hands so that you are able to hold onto him and ask him for help,
He gave you reason to get onto the path, to the sky

As reason is of the same make as the angels, it will take you towards him,
Like a hidden mirror in the palm of your hand, it will guide you (Rumi, Diwan-e Shams, Ode 3057)

Rumi says anyone who is not a lover, his appearance is as though he is living, but in fact he is dead.

Anyone other than the lover, is like a fish out water,
He is dead and lifeless, even if he is the holder of an important position (Rumi, Diwan-e Shams, Ode 1129)

The story of the dead tree

A gardener was cutting down the dead trees.

A dead tree said, "Why are you cutting me down young man? I have done nothing."

The gardener said, "Be quiet, what crime is worse than being dead."

Tree, "I am straight, not bent. Why are you cutting out my roots without any offence having been committed by me."

Gardner, "wish you were bent, but was alive and fresh. You would have then attracted the water of life and would have been part of the living. I have no animosity with you. Where ever I see any fruit sapling, I look after it like a mother, and cultivate it. Where ever I see a dead tree I cut it out, so that it is freed." (Masnavi, Book 6, Part 22)

A person who is living, he is "green", and is constantly growing. Greed, habits, addiction, and the like, block the way of growth. They dry the tree of any life. The person breaths, runs, puts effort in his activities, but does not, in fact, have any human life forces.

The one who is soulless becomes dead,
He becomes like an ass, if his soul is without that (spirit)

The one whose soul does not have that, is worthless,
this is the truth and Sufis have said it (Rumi, Masnavi, Book 4, Part 56)

PART IV: REASON

Rumi considers reason in the same way as love, to be the faculty by which we progress on the path to perfection.

Reason, love and cognition, became the ladder to the roof of the truth,
Although, in truth, the Truth, has another ladder (Rumi, Diwan-e Shams, Ode 384)

The specific quality of reason is "foresight"

I am Joseph, as is evident from my beautiful face,
No one asked the sun for any written statement as evidence

I am the tall cypress, which I can show you a sign of straightness,
There is no sign of more straightness, other than the cypress height

The witness of the moon is its beauty, goodness and joy,
The light of the stars is the witness and written statement of the sky

Hey you the flowers in the flower beds, who is your witness, the scent in the heads, and colours in the eyes?

If love is permitted to enter, what is the secret code of this permission?
It is: except for the face of the friend, nothing else exists

If reason is the judge, what is his Charter and Order?
It is: foresight, patience, honour and faith (Rumi, Diwan-e Shams, Ode 462)

The foresight of reason causes happiness.

*From the world, there are two opposing sounds, It depends ,
which one is compatible with you*

*One is, I am here now, and is shortsighted, The other, watches
the end, and is farsighted*

*Anyone who has foresight is happier,
Anyone who is shortsighted, is left alone and avoided by others*
(Rumi, Masnavi, Book 4, Part 61)

Rumi, not only considers reason being capable of detecting the
path and removing the obstacles with foresight, but also it
takes it as a director of our thoughts and emotions, which
manages and makes them organised.

*It is in human nature to have vengeance in anger, But reason
controls the ego with iron chains*

*It does not allow the ego to be active,
Reason is like a watch dog, whether it is over something
positive or negative*

*A faithful reason is just and fair,
It is the police, and the protector of the city of heart* (Rumi,
Masnavi, Book 4, Part 75)

 Reason is the wing and the feather of man, and setting forth
on any path without reason would result in failure.

*Pity goes to the featherless bird,
Takes the flight over the waves, and falls in danger*

*Reason is man's wings and feathers,
When he has no reason, he has no reasonable guide*

Without the key of wisdom, knocking on the door,

Is acting out of worthless desires (Rumi, Masnavi, Book 6, Part 116)

The man who does bad and evil things, is like a ship with no anchor,
To remain safe when the wind is in the wrong direction

For a wise man, the anchor is reason for safekeeping,
Learn this and request it from the wise (Rumi, Masnavi, Book 3, Part 208)

Reasonableness used by a number has the synergic, meaning, they strengthen each other's effect.

When one reason with another makes two,
Light is increased, and the path becomes apparent

Ego becomes happy and laughs with another ego,
When the wanting became plentiful, the way was hidden
(Rumi, Masnavi, Book 2, Part 1)

Soul is able to free reason from the slavery of the ego.

Hey, you, reason can conquer the sense, Also know that spirit can conquer reason

The closed hand of reason is freed, by the soul,
It resolved the problems to solution (Rumi, Masnavi, Book 3, Part 79)

SPECIAL QUALITIES OF REASON

Rumi regards three specific characteristics for the faculty of Reason:

Cognition

Management and Control

Harmony

Cognition

Rumi sees reason, as the faculty which applies the discernment to know right from wrong, and make choices accordingly.

Management and Control

Rumi sees the faculty of reason, as a guide which its duties are to manage and control thoughts, emotions and acts in order to move along the path of growth. Foolishness occurs when, instead of proper application of reason, emotions and improperly chosen and reviewed beliefs, take over the decision making progress.

Harmony

Rumi believes that attending to the Supreme wisdom and Reason, and harmonising with it, would determine the proper destination of the path of life, happening every moment, and would result in happiness.

CHAPTER SEVEN: THE COGNITION

The word cognition comes from the Latin verb cognosco ('con' meaning "with" + 'gnosco' meaning "know"). Broadly it's meaning is "to conceptualise" or "to recognise". *(Wikipedia)*

The subject of "cognition", has been studied in different areas of science and education, such as psychology, theory and philosophy of languages, computers and philosophy for many years.

Our abilities or weaknesses in correct cognition and conceptualisations, can affect the level of our success in life, and our happiness, satisfaction and contentment. We will consider, in this scroll, three main topics which are directly related to our cognitive powers, namely, problem-solving, decision-making, and emotions.

Every day, we face problems and difficulties in our daily activities, and we have to find solutions for them. These problems can be related to trivial mattes, or can be about serious and important matters. Irrespective to the size or the importance of the problem, there are two main realities, namely:

1. Life is filled with events and problems.

2. The secret to success and progress, is to solve these problems.

Whether we like it or not, problems do exist in our lives and we will always be facing them. Weak responses and running away from problems, will have disastrous results. Facing and solving problems, however, will act as a ladder to positive growth. Anyone who is capable of solving problems, whether related to family or personal matters, or related to work, society, finances and the sort, will be more successful.

Diagnosis of problems, and effort needed to solve them, are cognitive processes. The more we are able to properly cognise, the better we are in tackling problems and solving them.
The result is more success.

The next important subject which is directly affected by cognition, is decision-making. Two points are certain: First: whatever we are and we have at the present moment, is as a result of decisions we have made in the past.

Second: "cognition" is the foundation of decision-making. Anyone who makes a decision, initially he or she looks at the consequences of potential and probable decisions, and through this process, arrives at a final choice.

The decision-making process, which consists of seeing the consequences of the potential decisions, and making a choice between them, is totally dependant upon cognition. It is clear that the more our cognition is precise, accurate and closer to the reality, the better is the final decision.

The third subject, is the role of cognition in creating emotions. If we accept that the cause of our emotions is our take and understanding of the situations, and not the situations themselves, then by changing our views, we are able to change our emotions.

Thoughts are the creators of emotions, and we are able to change our thoughts. These are the two main pillars which cognitive therapy uses in order to treat problems associated with depression, fear, bipolar, abnormal sensitivities and other mind-problems of the sort.

In the cognition scroll and it's associated exercises, in an effective way, the cognitive abilities in the reader are improved. This improvement results in the strengthening of responses to problems and improving the ability to make sound and correct decisions.

THECOGNITION SCROLL

The story of the lake, the fishermen and three fish

Once upon a time three fish were living in a lake. One fish was wise, the other half-wise and the other stupid. One day a few fishermen were passing by and spotted the fish. The three fish also saw the fishermen. The wise one decided to swim towards the sea with haste. This was a difficult task and an unwanted event.

The wise fish thought to himself that he should not discuss his plan with the other two, as they would certainly try to dissuade him from doing it. This was because their love and dependance of the lake had made them lazy and their laziness and foolishness might have had an effect on him.

Consult matters with those who are free and not ruled by their ego

O, You traveler, consult with one who is into travelling,
as the one who is not, will dissuade you of it (Rumi, Masnavi, Book 4, Part 83)

The wise fish began to escape and as it was doing so, said to the other two, "I am going. You also should run away before the fishermen come back". So he went and the other two remained.

The fishermen returned and closed the exit from the natural lake with nets. The half-wise fish realised, there was no way to escape. He blamed himself and thought how foolishly he had behaved. He should have followed his wise friend. He should have escaped with him.

He then said to himself, there was no time for sad feelings and he should instead try to save himself. Suddenly he thought of something, "the best act is to pretend I am dead".

Floating on water, as though I am dead, surrendering my will,
dying before death is a safeguard from troubles (Rumi, Masnavi, Book 4, Part 87)

Pretending he is dead, he surrendered himself to the water. One of the fishermen was annoyed when he saw this, saying, "what ashamed! the better fish died". When the fish heard this, he became happy, saying, "brilliant! My plan is succeeded. I am saved."

Suddenly one of the fishermen got him out, spat at him, and threw him on the ground. The fish secretly and discreetly crawled to the water and disappeared.

The stupid fish felt the danger and began to jump up and down to escape from the bate, but the fishermen joyously caught him.

They laid the trap and caught him,
his stupidity was the cause of him being placed on the fire

In the frying pan on the fire, he slept with his foolishness

As they were about to cook him,
his reason told him, did I not warn you? (Rumi, Masnavi, Book 4, Part 87)

He accepted and told himself, if I manage to get out of this dreadful situation, I will never reside in a small lake again. I will choose nothing but the sea as my home.

I seek the infinite water and be safe,
for ever I move about safely and prosper (Rumi, Masnavi,
Book 4, Part 87)

The wise is a natural leader, due to carrying with him the light
of reason.   He lives in the present moment and does not
respond slavishly to events.

Like the wise fish before any decision, I rise above the
situation, and directly, without any emotions, beliefs, or value
judgement obstructing my views, I face matters, and then
decide on my course of actions.

Each event is an opportunity for the wise. The coming of the
fishermen was the golden opportunity for the wise fish to
understand the troubles ahead and the danger he was in. This
was in turn, the cause of him achieving his freedom, and
leaving the lake for the sea.

The one who is in the state of half-wisdom, does not have the
light of reason, like the wise, but is able to become
reasonable.

Even though his decision making process is not entirely under
the influence of reason, by imitating death, he gets rid of the
ego, albeit momentarily, and he manages to get out of danger.

When my ego has made my inner self dark and has covered the
light of reason, I get rid of the current, charging the ego, and
bring its activities to rest. Once the walls of the ego are
destroyed, I become free.

The wise fish went to the sea with the assistance of his reason,
and the one with half wisdom went to the sea with his chosen
pretence of being dead.

But what is to be said about the state of the fool? In his state, neither there is reason to guide him through the way, nor is he able to identify a reasonable path like the half-wise fish.

He is totally dependant on his ego, to the extent that his useless beliefs, emotions, greed and anything other than reason rules him. The wise and the half-wise, are able to see the reality before the event results in destruction, but the fool becomes aware of the same after, when it is too late.

The wise sees the consequences, and takes the initial stages of sorrow to the core of his soul, whereas the fool does the same in the final stages of sorrow.

When you have sorrow embrace it with love,
From the hill top view the beauty of the flatland of Damascus
(your destination)

The wise sees from the grape, the wine, The lover from nothing sees everything

Because the labourers could see there was profit in the painful carrying of the heavy loads,

They were all fighting over doing the job (Rumi, Masnavi, Book 3, Part 179)

Everyone has one way or another, experienced foolishness. In fact a wise man is not one who always acts reasonably, but he is the one whose foolish acts are a lot less.

From today I take anything that happens, as an opportunity for expanding and widening my comfort zone, and with the guidance of the light of reason, I proceed to discover my new land.

If there was no light, I will die, to end being ruled by my ego, and I sweep away the obstacles to achieve freedom.

If I am hurt by the acts of my ego, after recovery I will try to move away from that environment so that I would not be hurt again. This is to say, I will not repeat the same mistake. If it is repeated, I would not repeat it again, as each step towards the beloved, no matter how insignificant, is not without results.

The story of the wise and the snake

There was a wise man on a horse passing by a man who was asleep. He noticed a snake which was going into the sleeping man's mouth. The wise man quickly ran to cause the snake escape, but it was too late. The snake had totally gone into the sleeping man's mouth.

As he was a wise man, he often found a solution using his reason. He paused a moment and suddenly a thought came to him. With the whip he was holding, he threw a few slashes at the sleeping man.

The man suddenly jumped out of his sleep. The wise man with repeated slashes, managed to move him to a nearby apple tree. The wise man then pointed to the rotten apples on the ground and said, eat!

Why should I eat them and who are you?, said the man. The wise man said, either you will begin to eat them immediately or I will hang you from this tree right now.

He fed the man with so much rotten apples that some pieces of apples were dropping out of the man's mouth.

The man said, what sins have I committed that you are treating me like this? If you have old vengeance against me, you might as well strike me with your sword and end my suffering.

The wise man got on his horse and with his whip gave a few slashes to the man and said don't speak and now run.

The man, started running and he continued to curse the moment the wise man had passed by, saying, "I wish I had never seen you. What sins have I committed? What harm have I caused you? You are sick, you thug.". "Grant me my rights against this cruel man and punish him", he asked God.

Each time he stopped running, the wise man would administer more slashes, and would order him to run. He would continue to run, cursing and swearing at the wise man.

Suddenly the man felt sick, and what ever he had eaten he vomited. This also, included the snake. When the man saw the snake, he forgot all his pains and bowed to the wise man.

He said you are the prophet of love and kindness. You are either God himself, or his substitute. What a blessed moment it was when you saw me. I would have been dead and you gave me a new life. You were like a kind mother behind me, and I was escaping from you like an ass.

Lucky is the one who sees you. Oh great King, forgive my foul mouth and dreadful words I used, due to my ignorance. Oh dear King, if you had hinted to me about the snake being inside of me, I would not have used those dreadful words. I would have worshipped you and been kind to you.

The wise man said: If I had made the smallest hint about the snake you would have lost consciousness out of fear.

Many happenings in our lives which drag us into a hole, even though they appear to be upsetting and painful, they are character building.

From today, I see each person in my life as my teacher, and each happening as an opportunity to learn a lesson.

The story of the elephant in darkness

There was a city where its people had never seen an elephant. An elephant was brought to this city from India, and was taken inside a dark room. People were then invited in for viewing. The people were not able to see the elephant in the darkness.

They had no choice but to touch and feel the elephant with their hands. The one touching the trunk said: An elephant is like a large pipe. The other touching the ear said: An elephant is like a fan. Another touching the leg said: An elephant is like a pillar, and the other touching the back thought it was like a bed. Each thought of the elephant as that, which they had imagined.

Understanding and imaginations of each was different in relation to the elephant, and their descriptions were different. If each was carrying a lit candle, their differences would have disappeared.

Understanding made through a sense, like the sense of touching by the palm of one's hand, is defective and incomplete. One cannot cognise everything by senses.

Due to the diverse viewing their descriptions differed, one called it D, and the other A

If each was carrying a lit candle, the differences in their descriptions would have disappeared

The eye of the sense-perception, is only like the palm of the hand,
which has no power to reach the whole of him

The eye of the sea is one thing and the foam another, leave the foam and look with the eye of the sea

the foams move on the sea surface night and day,
you see continuously the foam and not the sea. This is
strange! (Rumi, Masnavi, Book 3, Part 49)

We don't see with our eyes, we don't hear with our ears, and we do not feel with our sense of touch! Our brain gets information from these senses, and in accordance with our beliefs they are interpreted and analysed. That, which sheds light to the mind and causes the reality to be cognised, is reason.

The Story of the Fly

A fly reached a puddle filled with donkey's urine. It happily landed on a piece of floating straw and as it was looking afar, like a captain on a ship, saying: "I have learnt a lot about ships and the sea, and have dreamt, for some time, that one day I would captain a ship, and now here I am".

"On the sea, in a ship and a knowledgeable me", he proclaimed, as he sailed over that infinite sea, floating his ship with pride.

That puddle filled with urine appeared to him as an infinite sea,
where was the vision which would see the reality

His world is as big as his vision,
This is the same for the eyes which see as big as several oceans
(Rumi, Masnavi, Book 1, Part 60)

The unreal understanding of the fly, taking a puddle filled with urine as sea, was due to his limited and wrong belief about the sea. Rumi tells us , the world of one man is as big as his beliefs. Many of our beliefs can be limited and wrong.

Rumi is pointing to an interesting and important concept in this story. He says, if the fly put his beliefs before others for critical discussions, he will be transformed into a phoenix and would no longer be a fly.

fly would be no longer a fly, if he learns this lesson,
that its spirit is not the same as its shape and form (Rumi, Masnavi, Book 1, Part 60)

Rumi, attributes happiness, greatness and power to having

proper cognitions and correct beliefs. The one who has the right cognition, has also correct judgment. The one with correct judgment, would also have the correct exercise of discretion in the decision making process, and would succeed in anything he does.

In order to have the right and proper cognition and beliefs, Rumi gives us simple and effective methods. Put your opinions and views before others, for debate and discussions.

Many times others' point of view saves one from wrong thinking.

From today, before making any decisions, I will pull myself above the situation and view the matter from that position. I will share the intended decision with those I trust and respect.

The story of the camel and the Mule

One day a mule saw a camel and said to him: I fall down to the ground all the time in the desert, in the slippery market place, and particularly when I am going down a hill. My face gets scratched and bleeds. Sometimes I also topple over my load, and it falls over my head, and I get whipped by my owner.

You Camel, however, how do you do it? The mule continued. You go to these long journeys, crossing fields, hills, riversides, deserts, and the like, and you hardly ever fall down.

The camel said: The precision of my sight is better than yours, my neck is longer, and I am able to see the whole journey from the above, and consider the ups and downs of the road.

Each step I take with correct and clear vision, I escape the falling and the stumbling

Whilst you see the immediate two or three steps ahead, you only see the bait and not the suffering of the trap (Rumi, Masnavi, Book 3, Part 76)

The mule said: You are absolutely right, and began to cry. I don't have a precision of sight and don't have a long neck.

The camel said: don't worry friend! In order to do the journey properly and be safe, you don't need a long neck. You should be able to see the whole journey from the above.

Before taking a step, rise above yourself and see the whole journey with all its highs and lows, and if you view without judgement, your vision will also be precise.

CHAPTER EIGHT: THE ANAGEMENT

Emotions play a very important role in our lives. They can change our thoughts and behaviours and can affect our cognitive abilities and decision making processes. Also many of our activities and their associated expenses, are to avoid certain emotions or gain other emotions.

Hence, the understanding and the management of our emotions, not only adds to our success in different areas, but also it can make us happy.

Generally, people use behavioural and cognitive strategies in order to manage their emotions. For example, doing exercises for feeling fit and well is a behavioural strategy or analysing an event which has caused anger is a cognitive strategy.

Rumi's method for the management of emotions is mainly based on cognitive strategy. In this scroll, the reader will become familiar with Rumi's constructive method. Rumi regards emotions as servants delivering messages, which their activities are necessary for our progress and development. He considers the appropriate response to emotions to be threefold, namely, acceptance, listening and ushering them away.

The readers, by reading the metaphors in this scroll and doing the exercises in the management of emotions, can use various emotions in a constructive way in their lives.

THE MANAGEMENT SCROLL

The Guesthouse

Rumi uses a simile, whereby our emotions, thoughts and ideas become messengers and guests, entering the house of our mind every moment.

Every moment, a thought like a dear guest comes in your mind

O you, dear one, regard the thought as a person,
because a person has his worth from his thoughts (Rumi, Masnavi, Book 5, Part 175)

Each thought and feeling has a specific message and duty. For example sorrow comes to sweep the dwelling of the mind, and make it ready for greater and deeper happiness.

Even though, the thought of sorrow occupies the place of happiness, it is preparing the mind for other happiness

It sweeps the house hastily clear of all else,
so that a new joy arrives from a blessed origin

It scatters the yellow leafs from the bough of the heart, in order for the connected green leafs grow

Whatever sorrow sheds from the heart or takes,
It is replaced, in truth, with better (Rumi, Masnavi, Book 5, Part 175)

I open my arms to entertain all my thoughts and feelings. I hear their messages and I then send them on their way.

Thought comes in the mind anew,
go to meet it with smiles and laughter

Respect the sour face thought, consider that sour, as sweet as sugar

If the cloud appears to be sour faced,
it is the bringer of the flower gardens and gets rid of salty and barren earth

Know the sad thoughts as the clouds,
do not look so sourly at the sour (Rumi, Masnavi, Book 5, Part 175)

Any thought and idea should be accepted like a very dear and valuable guest. It makes no difference if it is of sad feelings, disappointments, and fear, or of happiness, desire or dream. Each thought can bring with it a golden ideal, or be a blessed warning.

Perhaps that gem is in his hand, Endeavour so that he leaves you satisfied

Even if that gem was not in his hand, You will strengthen your good habits

That habit, elsewhere would benefit you,
and at another time, your need will be satisfied

Any little thought which hinders your joy,
there may be a hidden wisdom and an order in it

Stop reading it as worthless you young one, it may be bringing good fortune for you

Don't say it is a side issue and irrelevant, you consider it as main issue and relevant, so that by using it, you would achieve your goal.

If you consider it as a side issue and harmful,

your eyes will be waiting for the main issue

Poison came with the expectation of being tasted, you would constantly die if you use this method

Consider it as the main and stay with it,
stop this continuous deadly waiting (Rumi, Masnavi, Book 5, Part 175)

If I am dependant on specific thoughts, I spend most of my time in a state of waiting. For example if I like happy thoughts, I keep away from thoughts creating anxiety.

Whenever thoughts of anxiety come forward to bring their message to me, I distance myself from them and continue to wait for happy thoughts, whereas the main message, in the moment, was in fact the thoughts of anxiety which I kept away from me.

From today I will not label any thoughts or feelings. I will accept them all. One of the reasons which causes people to not to accept thoughts and feelings, is fear. Fear of inability to overcome them.

In some people, when they open the door to sorrow, sadness ends up ruling them rather than their reason. Their mind ends up covered in darkness. This is our problem rather than that of the emotions!

Reason! as the ruler of the mind, must accept them as guests, and not as the owner and occupier. Even if, due to necessity, they want to stay in the mind, they should be ushered to their rooms.

The Beauties

Learn this alchemy from a wise man, that whatever happens to you accept it

When you accept what has happened,
that moment, the doors of heaven are opened to you (Rumi, Diwan-e Shams, Ode 2675)

Suffering will arise when you want something which you don't have. Suffering can be beneficial and could cause revelations. It can also be tiring and crippling. The way to address suffering, is to determine its benefit and its destructiveness.

Beneficial Suffering

The creator of everything in the world is need. Without need there are no motivations and no actions. Nothing will be made. Need is the creator of the dreams. Need is the creator of power. It is the creator of enjoyment and wealth. Need is the creator of the object of the need. Whatever you have at present, whatever you like to have, and whatever you are doing at present, arises out of and is connected to a particular need.

How does need move us towards our goal?

It does so by suffering. Suffering is the child of need. Rumi in Fihi Ma Fihi tells us: "It is suffering which guides us, in whatever we are doing. Whatever the task, unless the suffering of the act and the love of the work, overwhelms him, he will not have any purpose for doing it, and without the pain and suffering, he will not succeed. It would be the same if the task is related to worldly matters, the blessed Kingdom to come, trade, the ruling of an Estate, science, astronomy, or anything else. "

The pain and suffering which moves us towards our goal and makes our positive talents to blossom, is a constructive or believing suffering.

The destructive Suffering

The destructive suffering is one which would not lead to motivation to do the acts. In other words, it is disbelieving. It is like a door bell which constantly rings, without resulting in the opening of the door. When we accept the pain and suffering and the situation we are in, we put our first steps forward, towards the solution of the problem. With this act, automatically the destructive suffering is transformed into a beneficial one.

Courage

If sadness is bringing you a message, meet it as an acquaintance

When the beloved is not behaving well, pleasantly respond with kindness

Until the vale is uncovered,
regard it as covering a sweet-heart beauty

Touch the vale and uncover,
see the teasing beauty hidden under the vale

In this like manner, I remain the lover, uncovering the vale of any beauty

All covered under the ugly vales, makes one think they are demons

I am not frightened, I am a demon lover,
You will understand this message, if you are the same

Sorrow will not see me, in any other state, but smiling,
Because, I regard the suffering as a medicine

There is nothing more blessed than sorrow,
as its rewards are unlimited (Rumi, Diwan-e Shams, Ode 2675)

Emotions are beautiful, attractive and soft angels who, when unknown, can be frightening and upsetting. When with courage you accept, observe and cognise them, they make their message heard and you will be able to see their beauty.

This courage is nourished from two sources according to Rumi:

1. Done with life approach: Rumi says I am done with this life. Therefore this man is not frightened of death.

2. Demon Lover

When we are "done with life", fear of death, as an obstacle, is removed. However, there is another obstacle, and that is the fear of the actual demon. Rumi, gets rid of this fear, by embracing and loving the demons representing those emotions. He greets them with open arms and embraces them.

False Emotions

A blind man was walking and suddenly a drunken man punched him. The blind man thought he was kicked by a camel, because he heard the sound of a camel at that very moment. He, then thought it must have been a pebble which was thrown at him. He was thinking of all kind of causes.

It was not this, it was not that,
That, which caused the fear, also caused this wondering

When he is not able to see the real cause, He is afraid of all kinds of things

Fear and shock arise, when the causes remain unknown,
No one is frightened of their own self (Rumi, Masnavi, Book 6, Part 76)

Imagining various causes, is because of not knowing the real cause. Thoughts and emotions can also carry false messages. Just because there are physical signs of anxiety, such as perturbation of the heart or being short of breath, it does not follow that there is, in fact, true anxiety in the system.

This is because there are many reasons which cause anxiety. Senses are able to cheat us. That, which is able to discriminate between true and false thoughts and emotion, is reason.

As was stated, each emotion carries a message. However, at times these emotions are false. Emotions have very close relationship with the faculty of cognition and the nervous system. When there is, no proper cognition of the events, or some interference with the nervous system, false emotions are produced.

Improper cognition is made when the reality of the situation is not seen. For example, a person may take someone's loud speaking, as a threat. This causes the person feel fear and anxiety. Someone else, may perceive the same situation, as the person being discourteous. This would then cause him annoyance or anger.

False emotions may also be caused by the physical factors within the body, such as disturbance within the nervous system, hormone imbalance, or genetic and physiological changes.

One of the most important factors in the successful management of emotions is to be able to discriminate between true and false emotions.

CHAPTER NIGHT: THE HARMONY

The third specific characteristic of reason, after cognition and management of emotions, is harmony. Not being harmonious could lead to shock, denial, anger, depression, feeling of being sacrificed, weakness, wrong decision making and helplessness. On the other hand, being harmonious and living in harmony with the universe, can result in happiness, power, internal satisfaction and self control.

According to Rumi, harmony has four main aspects:

1) Acceptance
2) Being in the present moment
3) Being in an appropriate role
4) Going forward towards the beloved or an ideal situation

Acceptance

Rumi believes that at any given moment anything could happen to us. It can be positive or negative. For example, death of loved ones, accident, falling in love, sickness, losing respect, becoming a hero, attaining self-consciousness, getting addicted, becoming a patent, becoming freed from incarceration, or getting convicted, winning the lottery and so on.....

Also that, it is possible for anyone to be anything, or to be in any situation, at any given time. For example, being oriental, black, or white, woman or man, bisexual or homosexual, blind, sick or healthy, rich or poor, born out of wedlock or not, abused or born and brought up in a warm and loving home, and so on.....

Once we accept our past and the situation we presently are in, we have taken the first steps in being harmonious. Acceptance does not mean agreeing with the situation or the condition. It is to accept the reality, in order to pass through it and move forward.

Being in the present moment

Those who do not accept the situation they are in, or their past, or they deny them, they live in the future. Those who have accepted their past as a forced pre-determined event, and have agreed with what has happened, are living in the past.

Being in the past or the future does not allow us to see the reality of the present moment. It reduces one's constructive energy and makes us lose the opportunities to deal with the life events appropriately.

Rumi believes we are born anew in every moment and the same applies to the world. We are not the same as the person of last year, nor are we the same as the person of a minute ago. Our surrounding environment and the world are also changing every moment.

A person who is living in the past or the future cannot choose the appropriate responses to these changes. He or she is like a doctor who writes a prescription before examining the patient.

Being placed in an appropriate role

Acceptance and being in the present moment are not sufficient for living in harmony. It is necessary to respond appropriately to any given situation. Each situation requires its own appropriate response.

For example, in certain situations we are required to be protective parents, or there are situations when peace is the only solution, whereas sometimes retaliation and war is the only option. Anyone or any country which has limited number of roles to play according to different situations, has reduced its survival rate and the rate of its progress and development. On the other hand, those capable of taking up many different roles, have much higher chance of survival, progress, and development.

Going forward towards the beloved or the ideal situation

Rumi believes the universe is moving in haste, towards perfection. In order to be harmonious with the universe we have to also choose the path to perfection. In order to be consciously on the path, we must have dreams and plans.

Rumi says, we must become like a skilful gardener and design the garden of our life, and have in our mind the ideal designed garden as our dream, so that when we view ourselves from the standpoint of the end of our lives, we appear to have lived a happy and fulfilled life.

The scroll of harmony, looks at subjects such as destructive information and habits, how to be in primary position when choosing the paths of life, harmony and changes of perception. There are exercises which the readers can do, to assist with the understanding of the concepts involved in being harmonious.

THE HARMONY SCROLL

The desert and the learned man

A desert man had put two loads on his camel. One had sand in it an the other grain, and he was travelling. A learned man came across him and asked: What are you carrying in those bags? The desert man replied, in one there is sand and in the other there is wheat grains!

The learned man: Why sand?

The desert man: I have filled one bag with sand so that it balances the weight of the grain.

The learned man suggested that he should empty the sand and divide the grains equally in either bags so that there would be balance, and the camel would not be carrying excess weight for nothing.

The desert man found this suggestion very useful. He then continued to talk to the learned man and found him to be very knowledgeable. He said to himself, he must be an important man, and asked him if he wanted a ride on his camel.

After a while, the desert man said: Tell me about yourself. How come with such knowledge, you are on foot, wearing such poor clothes?

The learned man did not reply. After they went along some more distance, the desert man said: I am sure you are a king or a minister traveling anonymously!

The learned man replied: I am neither a king, nor a minister. I am just an ordinary man.

The desert man said: So you must be a land owner. How many camels and cows have you got?

The learned man replied: I have no camels or cows.

You must be a tradesman, said the desert man. In your warehouse, how much fabrics have you got?

The learned man explained he had no shops or warehouses.

Oh I understand, said the desert man, you are an investor. How much cash have you got? You are an important man, having a lot of knowledge, your advice is with reason, and you travel alone. Anyone who has such knowledge is prosperous.

The learned man said: Believe me; I have nothing, except my daily food. I have no animals or clothes. I don't claim any ownership over my knowledge, reason or art.

Suddenly, the desert man said, get off my camel. You and your reason are a curse. Get away from me, as I may be contaminated by your bad spirit. If one bag of mine was loaded with sand and the other with grain, it was better than you, a useless man, loading my camel.

My foolishness are blessed ones,
when my heart, mind and soul are together in balance

If you want your pains be lessened, diminish your knowledge

A Thought is that, which opens a way,
The way is that, which we become a king in it (Rumi, Masnavi, Book 2, Part 92)

Knowledge and information are only necessary and beneficial when they solve problems, remove obstacles, and open doors to our problems. A knowledge which does not solve a problem, becomes another problem.

Knowledge and information which are useless should be discarded, as they would become an amusement, leading to disbelief and a waste of time. Also, any knowledge which is not a problem solver, gives us a false sense of self-satisfaction, eliminating the need in us, to seek necessary and beneficial knowledge.

Rumi, regards religions, schools of thoughts, ideologies, and the like, as a path. The path is only fruitful when it blossoms the positive talents in those taking it, and becoming transformed into a brilliant man (a king). Otherwise, those religions and schools of thoughts, are nothing but a waste of time and life. A vehicle for missing brilliant opportunities.

From today, in accordance with my needs, I read, hear, see and learn. Today, I will look at any religion, school of thoughts, methods and ways, from outside inwards, and observe the result of the training. I will choose my path with awareness and not by trial and error.

The stupid intelligent prince

A king put his young son in the hands of a group of learned and educated men, who taught him science, astrology, arts and the sort. They managed to turn him into a competent master at his young age.

One day the king, in order to test his son, put a ring inside his own closed fist and asked him to guess what he was holding.

The boy described what the king was holding as round, yellow, and hollow in the middle.

The King asked him to guess what the object was as the descriptions were correct.

The boy said, the object was a colander. How could you give such amazing signs of descriptions, and yet, the power of your knowledge and education was not capable of assisting you that a colander was not capable of being hidden in a closed fist, the king asked. (Rumi, Fihi Ma Fihi, Chapter 4)

Rumi considers the most important science and education we need is that of knowledge of the self. He believes, before attaining that, it is foolish to learn about other sciences. Cognition of our dreams is an important part of the path to self-knowledge.

Knows a hundred thousand things in science, But has no knowledge of his soul

You know the price of each item on the market,
If you don't know your self-worth, it is foolishness

The soul of all the sciences is this, and only this,
To know yourself when at the end of your life

Learning well the essence of all religions is good,
But better still is to learn the internal essence of yourself

The fundamental knowledge is that of the self,
So that you understand your true essence, O you, a fortunate
friend (Rumi, Masnavi, Book 3, Part 119)

Some people have to put a lot of effort, energy and time, in order to attain their goals in finance, job and family matters. More often than not, when we look at our achievements at the end of our life, those achievements are not what we really wanted. There was a lot of suffering and stress along the way and now too late to turn round.

Rumi says before putting any effort to achieve any goal, you should imagine you are old and you are looking at today, from that stand point. You then go ahead and design your life accordingly.

Just as a gardener, in order to grow the specific fruit from the tree, makes certain transplanting, we also have to have an imagination of the fruit of our own life. We then should act in accordance with the designed plan or order to achieve that end.

First thought came last in action, The world was created in this
way

The fruits were first in the thought of the mind, But in action
they appeared at the end

When you act, you have planted a tree,
At the end you read the first word (Rumi, Masnavi, Book 2, Part 23)

That which gives meaning to your life and makes you prosper, is not just dealing with religious matters, learning sciences or new skills. It is to live consciously in accordance with a system which you have chosen wisely.

Rumi believes that the whole universe is in motion in accordance with a mission. Our personal mission is only chosen wisely when it is in harmony with that of the universe.

I died from being stone to become mineral, From mineral I became animal

I died from being animal and became man,
So why should I be frightened? When did I become less by dying?

I will then die of being a man,
I would rise in angels with wings

I will then be moving on from being an angel,
And everything would be nothing, except for the image and the direction of Him

In the next stage, I will die of being an angel I will be transformed into that, which is unimaginable

I will be nothing like sound,
And all will be returned to Him (Rumi, Masnavi, Book 3, Part 187)

Rumi believes that the whole universe is like a roaring river flowing in the reversed current. Each person's success is to be in harmony with this river. This has passed several epochs in the past and has some epochs ahead. We are presently in the fifth epoch.

This is the epoch for purity of man, having presence, blossoming positive talents, and becoming accomplished. In this period, ignorance would gradually give way to knowledge, ugliness to beauty, weakness to strength, slavery to freedom, and poverty to wealth.

There will be less obstacles along the way of attaining one's goals, and dreams will become reality. When we look at our life, to determine the mission, from the stand point of being at the end of our life, we should ask these questions:

Have I been in harmony with the positive personal growth?

Have my positive talents blossomed?

Have I become more pure?

Has my life assisted in making the world a better place?

Have I provided an environment for others to grow and blossom?

Harmony

Harmonisation is not solely related to the determination of the mission. As the universe is unfolding every moment, harmonisation should occur accordingly.

Rumi believes if we are sad and depressed it is because we are not in harmony with this unfolding Universe at any given moment. If we were in harmony, we would be joyful and powerful, and everything would become interesting and beautiful.

Whilst I am at peace with this Father,
This world becomes a paradise as I observe

Every moment a new face and a new looks,
As I see and observe new, boredom disappears

I see the world full of prosperity, Water falling off the still springs

The sound of the waterfalls are heard,
I get drunk in my consciousness and soul

The branches dance like umbrellas,
The leaves clap hands like being in a concert

These states are like the reflection of the light in a mirror,
covered by a rug, what it would be like if it was uncovered!

From a thousand things that I could say, I don't even say one,
As the ears are filed with doubt

Illusion says these are just wishful thinking,

Reason says No, I have experienced them (Rumi, Masnavi, Book 4, Part 124)

If one is not in harmony with this process, the world appears annoying and upsetting to him. On the other hand, when somebody is in harmony, this same world appears to him as paradise. For example when a person has an accident and breaks his leg:

When in an unharmonised state, he might say: This damn accident has stopped me from being at the seaside and swim and enjoy myself.

When in a harmonised state, he might say: What is the best thing I can do at present? What opportunities this situation has provided for me?

The necessary element for being in harmony, in the present moment, is acceptance of situations, and placing oneself in an appropriate role for a proper response to the situations.

PART V: THE EXERCISES

The exercises in all seven scrolls are presented in a variety of forms. They are divided into hypnotic exercises and cognitive behavioural therapy exercises. As self-hypnosis makes up the main part of these exercises, the exercise of progressive relaxation is placed at the beginning of the exercises. The progressive relaxation, places the individual in a trance state, which is needed for the effective use of the other exercises.

Progressive Muscle Relaxation

Progressive muscle relaxation is a recognised method in hypnotherapy. This technic is used to relax the mind and body and placing the person in a trance state. When you are in a trance state the effect of the exercises are much deeper than being in a normal state.

Lie down in a quiet and comfortable place. Place your left hand on the stomach and the right hand on the chest. Breath using the stomach muscles. With each breathing in, your left hand goes up and with each breathing out, it goes down.

As you are calmly and deeply breathing, imagine you are walking towards a destination on a beautiful country lane. Look at the trees on either side of the road and their colours. As you deeply breath, imagine you arrive at a beautiful place. Lie down there and watch the blue skies with the little scattered clouds.

As you are lying down and breathing deeply, imagine, with each breath, a piece of white cloud enters your chest and as you breath out, it gets out grey coloured, as though it is taking the poison out of your body. In fact with every breathing in, you are breathing oxygen. The more oxygen you get to your body and mind, the more calm your system becomes. Equally, the more carbon dioxide you breath out, the calmer would be you body and mind.

As you breath deeply, pay attention to your left foot toes. Feel them. Then pull your toes in and open them slowly. Now attend to the bottom of your left foot and your ankle. Again pull them in and let go slowly.

Whatever muscle you release and loosen, it gets relaxed. Now attend to the muscle in your left calf. Again tighten and let go slowly. Do the same with your left knee.

Now attend to the muscles in the left thy, and again tighten and loosen slowly. Each muscle that you relax in this way, not only it relaxes itself, but also it relaxes the muscles which were already exercised.

Now attend to your right foot, and pull in and let go of the toes. As you do this continue with the deep breathing and imagine that the white clouds enter the right leg. Wherever you feel these clouds in the leg, that part becomes deeper relaxed.

Attend to the bottom of your right foot and your ankle. Again pull in and let go slowly. Each time a muscle is relaxed, the other muscles already exercised, will become more relaxed.

Now attend to the calf in the right leg, and tighten it and let it go. With each breath pay attention to the white cloud that enters your legs. Attend to your right knee and tighten it and let go. Attend to your right thy and do the same. Now attend to the muscles in your waist and in your back along your spine. Tighten them and let go. Feel the muscle in the stomach, and tighten them and let go.

When you are tightening and loosening the muscles of the body, the relaxation of your legs becomes deeper. People feel the relaxation of the legs in different ways. Some feel a pins and needles sensation, and others a numb feeling. Some feel them as weightless and light, and others as heavy.

At the same time attend to the muscles in the back on the side, and the middle. Again tighten and loosen them.

Attend to the chest. When you do this, make your breathing deeper and slower. Whilst the muscles in the legs, waist, stomach, back and chest are being deeply relaxed, attend to the white cloud which enters the lungs. Feel this cloud moving to your legs, waist, stomach, back and chest, with each breath. With each inhale and exhale and the exit of the grey clouds out of the body, your relaxation becomes more and more deep.

Attend to the left hand fingers. Open them out and then loosen them. Whilst you are relaxing the hand, the relaxation in your legs, waist, back, stomach and chest become deeper. Pay attention to the left wrist and open it out and let go. Attend to the front and the back of the left arm and the elbow. Tighten them and slowly loosen them and let go. Also the muscle in the shoulder, tighten and loosen.

Now attend to the right hand fingers and open and loosen them. Do the same with the wrist. Open and loosen them. Then move to the front and the back of the arm and the right shoulder. Again tighten and loosen the muscles slowly and let go.

Before we get to the relaxation of the neck and the head, with each deep breathing bring the white clouds in the lungs and exhale the grey clouds out. Each time you breath, feel that peace and calm which has come into your body, and the pressure and upset which is going out. With each breath your peace increases.

Attend to the muscles in the neck, tighten them and slowly loosen them. Attend to the muscles in the chin and around the lip. Tighten them and then slowly loosen and open them. Imagine, every time, you feel the white clouds in your head, face and neck. Your thoughts become less colourful and calmer.

Tighten your eyelid and you eyebrow, and then loosen and let go. Frown and let go. Now with each deep breath, feel the white clouds move to the lungs, stomach, legs, waist, back, arms, neck, face and head, and then the grey clouds leaving when you exhale. Take twenty deep breath in this way and pay attention with each breath to the relaxation of the whole body.

The Polishing Exercises

Self hypnosis

In the palace, you reach a mirrored-surfaced door. Above it is written, "the Polishing area". You enter. You find yourself in a university. You take a lift. As the lift is going lower and lower, you feel more deeply relaxed.

You exit the lift at the basement level. There is a laboratory there, and people, wearing white overalls, are looking through microscopes. You place yourself behind a microscope and look through it at a sample. You tune the focus of the microscope, and begin to see the sample more and more clearly. Scientist, through these tools have discovered the cured most destructive killer diseases. You leave the laboratory and take the lift again, to go to the top floor. As you go up the levels, you feel lighter and lighter in yourself.

At the top floor, people are behind telescopes and looking out to the sky. They have realised that observation and knowledge, are the starting steps of conquering. You leave the university behind, and with each step, your relaxation becomes deeper. Each breath you take, you feel lighter.
You see a man, at the top of the stairs, looking far ahead. May be you can hear his voice, or perhaps he is indicating to you, to go up the stairs. You go up the stairs, counting them, one by one, "one, two, ...". Each step you take, in your sub-conscious you feel a strange sense of depth and expansion. You continue to go up the stairs, and once on the eleventh count, you are next to the man. You begin to watch, and see very strange things.

You see naked people, eating raw fish. You pay more attention, and one looks very much like you. In another image, you see the history of your predecessors. You see them as cannibals! They worshiped really strange things. Their behaviours appears very strange. The man says, "there is no need to be surprised. It is their environment which makes them".

As you view the images closer to the present times, the predecessor's acts and behaviours become more familiar and normal. May be you watch those events in history which you like.

May be you like to think, human beings are now civilised and no longer made out of the environment surrounding them. May be these are not your thoughts. Suddenly he says, "it is civilisation which creates culture, the way of life, habits, religions, and even your conscience".

You go down the stairs. May be you feel, the shock created in your sub-conscious. May be not. You take a deep breath, and with each breath your mind becomes calmer. As it becomes peaceful, you enter in a quieter and calmer area.

You sit on a bed made out of stone. You hear a sound. The sound is coming from above your head. You see a man sitting on a tree branch. You feel getting lighter and lighter. You see yourself sitting next to him. He is indicating to something below. You look. You see another "you", sitting on the stone bed!

You are surprised he is reading your mind and saying, "The one sitting there is not the real you. It is a stranger residing in your home".

Then he says, "don't worry. You have taken the first step in conquering yourself and becoming free. The first step for changing, is to see yourself from outside".

Replacement

You can choose from one of those who performed the polishing acts, to be your model. It makes no difference whether you choose Buddha, Marcus Aurelius, Ghazali, Rumi, Albert Alice or any other person you value.

Look at your chosen model. See the level of his/her motivation, interest and the depth of attention, given to the cleaning and wiping away the beliefs and destructive habit.

Enter the image and shake his/her hand and embrace him/her. Dissolve in him/her and get into his/her mould. In the image you now only see him/her doing his activities. You are inside him/her.

Now that you are inside him/her, you have his/her vision. What are your feelings?

How do you see your own inner being?

Watch yourself in your own life situations, and you notice your model comes towards you. He/she shakes your hand, embraces you and enters your mould.

Now that he/she is inside you, what are your feelings?

How do you see your own inner being?

You may remember this experience, or your conscious may forget it. Your sub-conscious stores this in your system, and during a recall, you feel this experience.

Conditioning

Feelings	Causes	Review of Causes	Checking Replacement	Replacement	Actions
Feeling perfect, Self-centredness	Embracing the Model and absorbing Has replacement been completed? Is replacement stable?	What are my thoughts and feelings? How do I think and feel?	What are my feelings now? Do I see my faults? Am I motivated to get rid of my faults?		

Whenever you feel perfect or are self-centred, deterministically do the replacement exercise. Answer the questions in column 2, to ascertain if you have correctly done the exercise. In the third column, answer the questions related to the results of doing the replacement. In the column headed, "review of causes", look for the probable cause of the emotions. Write the cause/s in the fifth column. Write the actions or the plan of actions in the final column, for eliminating the causes.

The Attention Exercises

Self hypnosis

Inside the palace you see a blue coloured door. It is written on it "attention". You enter and see a city. May be at first you don't see the images clearly or lively. May be you do. In any event, as you breath in and out deeply, the images become clearer.

You see a person standing on a higher platform and appears to be a leader motivating his listeners and giving a speech. You look at the faces of his followers, one by one, and the more you look the clearer and livelier their faces become.

You look at the face of the speaker. May be you don't hear his voice, but you are able to see in his face and by his actions the excitement, motivation and happiness, like flowing emotions.

Excitements and motivations create more excitements and motivations. Leaders are inspired by their dreams and get excited and motivated by them. The clearer are the dreams, the more they motivate and are fanciful. Our dreams are like our beloved, and we get energy from observing them.

As you proceed in this dreamland, you see a young doctor in his room, who has attached a large piece of paper on the wall. It is written on it "less than 4 minutes". It is his dream, to run one mile in less than 4 minutes. Almost all the professionals consider this as impossibility. But this is the dream of this young doctor and he is steadfast in believing his dream.

Many things which are around you, are so normal such that they go unnoticed and taken for granted. One day they appeared to somebody as impossibility.

You step on a bridge. Each step you take your body is more relaxed. The images and what you feel become clearer and deeper. With each step you are closer to the end of the bridge.

You see your destination clearer and clearer. On that side of the bridge you see a lover who has his beloved's picture in his pocket. Even when he is not looking at the picture, he thinks about her. Even though the separation from the beloved is painful, the dream of seeing her and being united, gives him energy and excitement.

Anyone who has a dream is like a pregnant woman, who caries the foetus around. May be this carrying is not easy, or even difficult and painful, but most people spend their pregnancy period with feelings of happiness, excitements and look forward to the birth of their baby.

Replacement

You can choose amongst these leaders, lovers and those who have dreams, a model for yourself. It makes no difference. The leader's dream is his beloved, and the lover's dream is also his beloved.

Your model can be a professional sportsman. He either is doing training and exercises, or is communicating with his team and talking about his ideas and what he has learnt. May be your model is a public or a political figure.

He is also like the sportsman. He has colleagues who are communicating with him. He is in touch with his dreams and acting on them. May be your model is an artist or a historical figure. It really does not matter. One of the main characteristics of anyone who has fulfilled his/her dream, is attention.

Look at your chosen model. Look and see the level of his/her attention, with all the excitements and motivations given to his/her beloved or his/her dream. Go into the image and approach your model. Shake his/her hand and embrace him/her. You will dissolve in him/her and become his/her mould. In the image now you only see him/her being active and you are not there. You are inside him/her.

Now that you are inside of him, and see from his/her vision, how do you feel?

What do you think?

Watch yourself in your achievements and your successes in your life. You will notice that he/she (your model) comes to you, shakes your hand and embraces you. He comes into your mould.

Now that he is on you, what feelings do you have?

How do you think?

You may remember this experience or your self-conscious may forget it. But your sub-conscious will store this and during a recall it will be felt again.

Conditioning

Feelings	Causes	Review of Causes	Checking Replacement	Replacement	Actions
Low in motivation Lack of interest	Embracing the Model and absorbing Has replacement been completed? Is replacement stable? What are my thoughts and feelings? How do I think and feel? Who do I see?	What are my feelings now? Am I more motivated?			

Whenever you feel low in motivation and lack of interest, deterministically do the replacement exercise. Answer the questions in column 2, to ascertain if you have correctly done the exercise. In the third column, answer the questions related to the results of doing the replacement. In the column headed, "review of causes", look for the probable cause of the emotions. Write the cause/s in the fifth column. Write the actions or the plan of actions in the final column, for eliminating the causes.

The Wanting Exercises

Self hypnosis

In the palace the section for wanting is next to the section for attention. You can turn its red door knob and enter the atmosphere of wanting. You see a tower being built. In each part, a group of people are working.

You walk towards them. Each group have attached their work program sheet to the wall. As soon as a task is concluded, they put a tick in front of it and move onto the next task. Each person is carrying out his duty with such commitment, as though it is the most important piece of work in their lives. The towers have been built in this way.

You pass the workers and the red lights stops the cars. You cross the street. You go towards the uptown part of the city. With each step the relaxation in your body become deeper and deeper.

As you are going up the slope of a hill, you see someone is walking down the hill. From his manner of walking and his strong steps marching down, you get the impression that he is confident. He walks towards you and is holding a book.

He shakes your hand and you feel a type of strength and energy in yourself. He is a prophet and is going to execute his mission. Most prophets do not hesitate to do their duties and this is how great events in history have taken place.

You continue your journey, now with stronger and more determined steps. You see an archer ready to pull the arrow. His whole attention is on the aim. Professional archers at such a moment, see nothing else but the aim. You also momentarily hold your breath.

He releases the arrow and it hit directly the aim. You now concentrate and proceed on your path. You walk into a stadium, and in the athlete's ground, you see a young man doing training and running. After each round and session in his training, he goes to a notebook and ticks a box, written 3.59.9.

There are other ticks in the notebook relating to other exercises. His attention and dedication to his training is similar to the mission of the prophet. Your sub-conscious reaches a determination and steadfastness of such level which replaces your previous mode of operation.

Replacement

You can choose as a model one of these achievers. It makes no difference if he is a businessman, a manager, a scientist, a sportsman or a prophet. They all have something in common; Commitment. Their greatest asset is their commitment to complete the task at hand.

Look at the model you have chosen. See, with what motivation and determination he is executing his duties. Enter the picture you are observing. Shake his hand and embrace him. Dissolve in him, so that you are placed in his mould. You now only see him busy with his activities.

Now that you are inside and have his/her vision, what feelings do you have?

How do you make efforts?

Now look at yourself in your own life situations. You notice your model comes to you, shakes your hand and embraces you. He/she enters your mould.

Now that he/she is inside you, what feelings do you have?

How do you make your efforts?

You may remember this experience, or your self conscious may forget it. But your sub-conscious has stored it, in your system and it will be felt once it is read again.

Conditioning

Feelings	Causes	Review of Causes	Checking Replacement	Replacement	Actions
Low motivation in executing the plan Lack of interest	Embracing the Model and absorbing Has replacement been completed? Is replacement stable? What are my thoughts and feelings? How do I think and feel? Who do I see?	What are my feelings now? Am I more motivated?			

Whenever you feel low in motivation and lack of interest, deterministically do the replacement exercise . Answer the questions in column 2, to ascertain if you have correctly done the exercise. In the third column, answer the questions related to the results of doing the replacement. In the column headed, "review of causes", look for the probable cause of the emotions. Write the cause/s in the fifth column. Write the actions or the plan of actions in the final column, for eliminating the causes.

The Dying Exercises

Self hypnosis

You reach a green door, with the word "Dying" written on it. You enter and inside is a green and vegetated environment. There are saplings and green trees everywhere.

A beautiful river is flowing in the middle of the green fields and there are beautiful, colourful birds and exotic butterflies, flying happily around. With each breath in this wonderful, fresh atmosphere, you feel refreshed and happily peaceful.

You cross a bridge and begin to walk towards, what appears to be, an Island. The closer you get, the more the atmosphere is changed.

The green fields look as if they are drying out. The trees are less and less green. A lot if trees appear dead. The river is no longer flowing. The water is still, sludgy and smelly.

You see a man on the island. He is the lover, who had the picture of his beloved in his pocket, standing on the other side of the bridge. He is still alive, but has not been able to cross the bridge. He has no means of coming to the green side, other than crossing the water, or the bridge. He has phobia about both.

Majority of us, are prisoners of our fears.

The continued remaining of this man, this lover, on an island like a prisoner, or his freedom, depends on two types of power; the power of fear or the power of love. You turn away from the Island of death and face the city. You look at the sea and the city with its noticeable greenness even from such far distance.

With each step forward, you feel better. You look at the sky. The weather is cloudy. It looks as if, storm is on its way. You begin to run to a shelter. The wind is now blowing very hard. The sea is rough. The people under the shelter are pointing to the sea with anxious excitement. There is a boat in the sea. You zoom you camera on the boat to have a look. The person in charge of the boat is a person you recognise. He is the lover on the death Island. His face is full of life and hope.

Most audiences like films that have happy ending. Some are energised by the success of the hero of the film. Some feel more peaceful. May be you have both of these feelings now. May be you feel different. In any event, you step towards towards the city stadium, with more motivation.

Once at the stadium, you see the young athlete, doing his last session of training. Almost everyone agrees, that no one can run a mile in less than 4 minutes. It is practically impossible. But this young athlete believes it to be possible. He is a winner before the tournament. His aim is three minutes and fifty nine point nine minutes.

On 6th of a May 1954, there was astonishing news that a young man, by the name of Roger Bannister, 25 years of age, ran a mile in 3.59.4 minutes.

The interesting point was that Bannister's record only lasted 46 days. Another athlete also managed a mile in less than 4 minutes. Where were these runners up until that point in time?

What limits people, and stops their positive growth, is not solely dependant on their abilities. It is also dependant on their beliefs.

You reach the upper part of the city. It is placed above the hill. You look from the top of the hill towards the streets and people. You see their fears, habits and beliefs as hidden prisons without rails. Whilst you are thinking about these things, you hear the voice of the alchemist from behind you, saying: "we have easier and more powerful way for the entrapment or freedom of people".

You turn around and ask, "What way?"
The alchemist says: "you can entrap or free people easily by naming them. When you accept you are depressed, sick, addicted, man, woman, poor, Muslim, Christian, Buddhist, atheist, Japanese, African, European ...then you have identified and specified the limits of your prison."

What is the name which makes you free?

If you want to constantly pass through the limitations, and persistently grow and develop positively, the best name is to be a "lover"

The lives of lovers are in the dying,
You will not find the heart, except in the heart-slavery (Rumi, Masnavi, Book 1, Part
90)

Replacement

You can choose as a model one of these amazing and extraordinary people. It makes no difference if he is a businessman, a manager, a scientist, a sportsman or a prophet. They all have something in common. That is continuous growth and progress.

Look at your chosen model. See how deterministically and with what motivation he/she is passing through his/her comfort zone. Enter the image and shake his/her hand and embrace him/her. Dissolve in him/her and enter his/her mould. In the image now it is only him/her busy with his/her activities and you are inside him/her.

Now that you are inside him/her, you have his/her vision. What feelings do you have?

How effortful you are?

See yourself in your daily situations. You notice your model comes towards you. He/she shakes your hand and embraces you. He/she enters your mould.

Now that he/she is inside you, what feelings do you have?

How effortful you are?

You may remember this experience. Your conscious may forget it. Your sub-conscious feels it, when recalled.

Conditioning

Feelings	Causes	Review of Causes	Checking Replacement	Replacement	Actions
Stress Fearful Low in appetite	Embracing the Model and absorbing Has replacement been completed? Is replacement stable? What are my thoughts and feelings? How do I think and feel? Who do I see?	What are my feelings now? Am I more motivated?			

Whenever you feel under stress, or fearful, or are low in appetite, deterministically do the replacement exercise. . Answer the questions in column 2, to ascertain if you have correctly done the exercise. In the third column, answer the questions related to the results of doing the replacement. In the column headed, "review of causes", look for the probable cause of the emotions. Write the cause/s in the fifth column. Write the actions or the plan of actions in the final column, for eliminating the causes.

The Cognition Exercises

The exercise of five-Roles

Inside the palace, the cognitive centre is in a room. A team of five strong, are active at this centre.

The members of this team are the sun minister, the moon minister, hoopoe, the wind and the Gnostic.

The foundation of any correct judgement and decision, is having accurate and substantial cognition in relation to the subject matter. We can have accurate and correct cognition in relation to any subject matter, if we are able to view it from different angles. In this exercise, you will learn to view matters from five angles.

Positive thinking, with the symbol of the sun minister

Critical view, with the symbol of the moon minister

Information gathering, with the symbol of hoopoe

Foresight and viewing the conclusions, with the symbol of the wind

Intuitive thinking, with the symbol of the gnostic

Look at the subject matter. This method widens your vision, and makes it deeper. It strengthens your cognitive powers and assists you with arriving at the correct decisions.

Method of Operation

First get into each of the five roles, one at a time. View the problem from the stand point of each role. The better you understand the operation of each role, the more effective is this exercise.

To cognise any subject with this method, make the problem specific and clear. The hoopoe is sent to gather as much information as is needed. Then the sun minister, the moon minister, the the wind and the gnostic, in this order, announce their opinion.

The Sun Minister

The Sun Minister is the symbol of positive thinking and being optimistic. Positive thinking means seeing the glass half full. Those who are in a state of positive thinking, see the positive side of the world and they believe and have faith in reaching their aims and making their dreams come true. It is with positive thinking that people set out their aims and plan.

Benefits of the Sun Minister

- ✓ Excitement, joy and higher motivations
- ✓ More flexibility and higher power

The Moon Minister

The Moon Minister is a critic, and is a symbol of negative thinking. He sees dangers and what is lacking. The reality is that people do not achieve all their goals and their plans fail. Near high peaks, there are deep valleys. In nature spring is green and winter is cold. Most of our failures are in fact, due to not having enough Moon Minister in our thoughts.

Benefits of negative thinking

- ✓ Less mistakes
- ✓ Better decision making

The Hoopoe

Hoopoe elevates and views from the above. Not only he sees all details with precision, but also is able to see the depth and the inside. Hoopoe perceives matters without judgment and gathers information. For example, if he is asked to give information about a particular tree, he looks at the tree from above, and gives full information about the tree classified under separate headings.

Benefits of Hoopoe:

- ✓ Lack of negative effects of judgments
- ✓ Giving information and using past experiences

The Gnostic

A Gnostic is a symbol of intuition. He acts in accordance with the feeling he has in relation to that matter.

What is intuition?

Intuition is "the Inner knowledge, without the use of reason". It is a feeling about something which cannot be explained easily or proved. Sometimes we " only know" something "appears" to be correct, or sometimes we observe that something which " feels" to be wrong.

The Gnostic explains his feelings in relation to the intended decision. On the one hand, a Gnostic is a symbol of receiving ideas. In fact, anything discovered by human being in the world was initially just an idea in the mind.

Problems can have different or many solutions. One of the ways of achieving creative problem solving is to open the mind, and write down any solution or idea which comes to mind.

Benefit of the gnostic:

✓ Creativity
✓ Sensitivity

The Wind

Anything is made or destroyed in accordance to a set of rules. Reaching a goal, whether positive or negative, forms a unique path. Wind moves along the path, and is able to see the completed process. Once you view from the stand point of the wind, you see the whole of the path and the transformed processes.

For example: when you are in place of the wind, you witness the natural activities of a seed planted in the soil, and the whole process of transformation of the seed to a thick tree. Or, when you see someone who has just started using drugs, you are able to see his addiction in due course and his changes of personality.

Equally when you see a firm which starts expending and getting bigger and richer, you are able to see it turning into an economical giant.

Of course, processes may differ due to different factors. For example, the planted seed which is watered properly undergoes a different process to that which has not been nourished and watered properly. Wind sees the process and the effective elements and factors, and the end.

Benefits of the Wind:

- ✓ Widened vision
- ✓ Improved abilities to withstand difficulties

The exercise of planning (the separation of decision-making process and the execution of the plan)

This exercise is related to the specific characteristics of the wanting (scroll number 3). You make decisions and plan the actions in this exercise. When executing those duties, you act on what has already been planned.

Planning the daily activities and separating the decision-making phase to the execution phase, avoids waste of energy and time, and is more effective. For example, consider the driving rules and regulations. If there were no rules any driver, arriving at a junction, would have to decide whether to pass, remain, allowing the opposing side to cross, etc.

A great deal of the drivers' energy is consequently spent on continuous decision-making, whilst driving. This results in increased levels of stress and much reduced efficiency. In another example, take the construction of a tower.

Again the planning and execution are separated. If that was not the case, the work would never be systematic and the project would not be completed. Even if such operation is possible, it would take a lot of time at a great deal of expenses and costs.

In human related matters, this holds in exactly the same way. For example, a sportsman, who wants to be ready for a particular tournament, will have to do the same thing and separate the planning phase and the execution phase.

You can write your daily plans in whatever way you choose. It is important that by the time you are executing your duties, there is a plan of you actions in existence and that your activities are in accordance with that plan. It is good if the plan is written the night before.

The Management Exercises

Acceptance exercise

The acceptance exercise has three parts: acknowledgment and greeting the thoughts or emotion, receiving their messages, and ushering them out of the system. This exercise is done in the palace and the aim of it is to strengthen one's ability to accept thoughts and feelings, and using them. Duration of this exercise is five to ten minutes.

Management exercise

This exercise is done during the day and its aim is to manage thoughts and uncontrolled emotions. Duration of this exercise is two to five minutes.

Acceptance exercise

You are walking in the corridors of your large and beautiful palace and viewing the beautiful paintings, hung on the walls on either side of the corridor. May be you see clearly what is painted and see it as bright. May be you don't see it clearly and it looks dark. It may be that they become gradually clearer. As you view each painting separately and pay attention to its details your body becomes more relaxed.

The Relaxation of the body happens when one looks at and concentrates on the enjoyable sceneries in the paintings. Some people get relaxed by looking at the picture of a beautiful smiling child. Others get relaxed by looking at the picture of a sunflower field, or a sunny beach showing the waves of the sea.

The corridor of the palace opens to a beautiful big garden. In that garden there are beautiful colourful flowers of different kinds. May be the first flower you see is a rose. May be it is yellow in colour. Whenever you pay attention to the flowers you can see them more clearly.

As you are watching the flowers, a guest who has a message for you enters. May be you don't want to see some of these guests, such as, fear, anxiety, disappointment or depression. May be, when depression enters, it hangs dark curtains over the windows. May be it freely moves about the Palace and weakens the motivation of the others. May be, anxiety brings with it, worry and disturbance and affects others.

In order to receive the messages and maintain the joy and happiness of the Palace, do the following important acts:

1. Greet each thought or emotion with warmth and sincerity.

Each thought and feeling is carrying a message for you. If you ignore them or not properly receive them, they will go away without giving you the message. You would then have deprived yourself of receiving these potentially very important messages.

2. Manage that thought or feeling:

Any thought or feeling which is in free to move around in the house of your mind, can, at times, cause nuisance. Acceptance and warm greetings of any emotion or action, does not mean agreeing with them and allowing them to be free in the house of the mind. Once you have heard the message, you can warmly usher them out, or if they want to stay in the palace for a short period of time, to direct them to their rooms.

Go to the future, and with different thoughts and emotions, practice the technique of greetings and ushering away.

The guest of thought or emotion	Acceptance and greetings	Receiving the message	Follow up and action	Ushering away

Example

The guest of thought or emotion	Acceptance and greetings	Receiving the message	Follow up and action	Ushering away
Peace, cheerfulness and reasonable response	No evidence of intentional disrespect or evidence of disrespect was observed	Someone has been disrespectful and respect is one of my important values	done	anger
peace and confidence	with the decision making technique, review this idea	with the continuation of this talent situation, your time will be wasted. With the possession

of this firm, you will have more income. Independence and having an income are my

important values | done | The idea of opening an institution |
| | | | | |

Management exercise

Sometimes, these feelings and emotions, like duty bound servants, when they enter the Palace, they are turned into a devil and disturb the peace of the Palace.

Emotions become stubborn due to two main reasons:

1. When their message is not heard

2. When they are turned into a devil

Emotions are serious agents, and if they are not allowed in, or accepted, they bang on the door with their fists. If you accept them, but act indifferently towards them, and not hear their message, they will shout at you. If you get the message and don't act, they will remain.

If you get the message and follow it up and act accordingly, and still the emotion has stayed and has not left, it is turned into a devil. You can manage and control it by the following methods.

Rising

Emotions can be in charge and overcome and rule you, when you are in their domain. Once you rise above and elevate out of the situation, and see that feeling or thought along side of others, it would be you who would be in charge and in control. When you look from above, you see that feeling the same as others, coming and going in and out of the Palace. You can then come down and choose whichever emotion you want to speak to.

Exercise of Rising

Feeling	apparent signs	Rising	apparent signs after replacement

Example

Feeling	apparent signs	Rising	apparent signs after replacement
Depression	Sad, low energy, headache, low appetite	View the feeling from above	Lightness

Choosing The Opposite Emotion

This is to choose the opposite emotion to replace an emotion which is a nuisance. For example if the emotion which is a nuisance is sadness, then choose happiness. Or if happiness is causing headless joy, then choose sorrow. Also, when you are sad, and this is a false emotion which has turned into a devil, with doing happy acts, such as, singing, dancing, joking, you can do the replacing.   Opposing emotions, of course, eliminate each other.

Exercise

Feeling	apparent sign	Opposite emotion	apparent signs after replacement

The Harmony Exercise

Self hypnosis

You reach a purple coloured door. This is the harmony section.

You enter. By the side of the road, your favourite car is parked. You sit in the driver's seat. You re-arrange the seat. You take a deep breath and begin to drive. May be it is in the morning and it is just getting lighter. May be it is in late afternoon.

Whatever time of the day it is, you enjoy the drive down the beautiful road. The road bends, and you drive round the bend. When the road's conditions are appropriate, you overtake a car. You harmonise with the road and its conditions.

There are many divers, just like you, doing the same thing. On the road of life, there are fewer people, who harmonise with it.

Some of the "dos" and "don'ts", we use in our internal conversations, take us out of harmony.

We say, "This should not have happened".
Or, "he should have done this".
Or, "the situations must be as I want them".

This is like saying, "why is there a bend in the road? I want it to be straight". If you tolerate, and drive round the bend with annoyance, you will not enjoy your life's events. You also, do not leave the road either.

You park next to a roaring beautiful river. You see a number of people with their small colourful boats racing. You follow them with your eyes. You see those who harmonise with the currents in the river, are more successful.

You drive towards the city. You notice, the more you harmonise with the road, the more relaxed and patient you are. You reach Wall Street. You see the colourful posters of stocks and shares, and investment companies.

Behind this crowded, glittering and shinning appearance, the laws in investment and acquiring wealth, are hidden. These laws, like other original and effective laws, are so simple that they go unnoticed.

Success in the market is made, through adhering to two simple laws:

1. Get to know the spirit of the market

2. Harmonise with it

In fact it is just one law, "harmonise with the market".

You enter a large store. You try a number of garments in front of a mirror. May be you need something formal. May be something casual in black, blue or another colour.

Identities and roles are like these garments. Each are for a particular place, and purpose. Someone can be in harmony with the positions and the situations of life, who detached from any of these identities and roles. As he changes his outfits to suit a particular purpose, he changes his roles.

PART VI: TABLES

Each exercise table is designed for 14 days. Each table, has 3 questions, which should be answered three times a day.

Each question has a mark ranging from 0 to 3. At the end of each day, the marks are added. The maximum mark in two weeks is 210. If one is able to score 150 in two weeks, he or she can then be ready to go to the next scroll. If the total is less, the same scroll is repeated.

In the following a sample table of each scroll is presented. Readers can copy them to use as required.

THE TABLE OF THE FIRST SCROLL: POLISHING

Monday	Date	Total scores:	AM	Noon	PM
1. Did I read the Polishing scroll?					
2. Did I observe prejudicial behaviours in me?					
3. Did I observe myself being greedy?					
4. Did I do the conditioning exercises?					
5. Did I do the palace exercises and self-hypnosis?					

Palace exercises and self-hypnosis are done once a day and have 3 marks

THE TABLE OF THE SECOUND SCROLL: ATTENTION

Wednesday	Date	Total scores:	AM	Noon	PM
1. Did I read the scroll of attention?					
2. Did I go to my beloved and observe him/her, when unwanted temptations and emotions came over me?					
3. Were my words and acts as those of my beloved					
4. Did I do the conditioning exercises?					
5. Did I do the self-hypnosis exercise?					

THE TABLE OF THE THIRD SCROLL: WANTING

Monday	Date	Total scores:	AM	Noon	PM
1. Did I read the scroll of wanting?					
2. Did I act with motivation and excitement towards achieving my goals?					
3. Did I continue in my efforts when disappointed?					
4. Did I do the conditioning exercises?					
5. Did I do the self-hypnosis exercise?					

THE TABLE OF THE FORTH SCROLL: DYING

Monday	Date	Total scores:	AM	Noon	PM
1. Did I read the dying scroll?					
2. Did I accept my stresses with open arms?					
3. Did I widen my comfort zone at least a step wider?					
4. Did I do the conditioning exercises?					
5. Did I do the self-hypnosis exercise?					

THE TABLE OF THE FIFTH SCROLL: COGNITION

Monday	Date	Total scores:	AM	Noon	PM
1. Did I read the cognition scroll?					
2. Did I discuss them with others?					
3. Did I use them in my daily activities?					
4. Did I do the cognition exercise?					
5. Did I write tomorrow's plans?					

The cognition exercise is done once a day and has 3 marks

THE TABLE OF THE SIXTH SCROLL: MANAGEMENT

Monday	Date	Total scores:	AM	Noon	PM
1. Did I read the scroll of the management of thoughts and emotions?					
2. Did I accept my thoughts and emotions?					
3. Did I manage my thoughts and emotions?					
4. Did I do the management of thoughts and emotion exercises?					
5. Did I do the self-hypnosis exercise?					

THE TABLE OF THE SEVENTH SCROLL: HARMONY

Monday	Date	Total scores:	AM	Noon	PM
1. Did I read the scroll of harmony?					
2. Did I correctly realise the situations?					
3. Did I accept the situations?					
4. Was I in harmony with the situations?					
5. Did I do the self-hypnosis exercise?					

Printed in Great Britain
by Amazon